PADDY
COLE

PADDY COLE

King of the Swingers

With Tom Gilmore

THE O'BRIEN PRESS
DUBLIN

*This book is dedicated to my dad, Paddy Cole Snr., who taught me
to read music and play the saxophone. He also taught me, amongst many
other things, to drive a car, to fly fish for trout, and the true meaning of the
word Respect. He was my hero. I'm sorry I never told him!! – P.C.*

*Dedicated to the memory of my parents the late Katie (Lally)
and William (Bill) Gilmore. – T.G.*

First published 2020 by The O'Brien Press Ltd,
12 Terenure Road East, Rathgar, Dublin 6, D06 HD27, Ireland.
Tel: +353 1 4923333; Fax: +353 1 4922777
E-mail: books@obrien.ie. Website: www.obrien.ie
The O'Brien Press is a member of Publishing Ireland.

ISBN: 978-1-78849-221-8

8 7 6 5 4 3 2 1
24 23 22 21 20

Printed and bound by ScandBook in the EU.
The paper in this book is produced using pulp from managed forests.

Published in

DUBLIN

UNESCO
City of Literature

Contents

Foreword

Paddy Cole's earliest musical influences – like those of many of us – emanated from his home.

The Cole home in Castleblayney, County Monaghan, where Paddy's parents reared one son and six daughters, resounded to the sounds of old 78rpm jazz records. His father was an enthusiastic sax player. In his teens, Paddy's attempts at becoming a butcher, and later an electrician, were rather lacklustre, because his head and his heart merged with music.

Paddy has had a stellar career. His exceptional musical talent across all genres has entertained generations, nationally and internationally. He joined The Capitol at the dawn of the showband era, a period that would coincide with the emergence of global legends such as Elvis Presley, The Beatles and The Beach Boys. Recognition of Paddy's unique musical talents spread from Ballybunion to Ballybofey ... and were the envy of other bands.

As the showband era entered its sunset, Paddy moved to Las Vegas with Brendan Bowyer, Twink and Tom Dunphy. They were The Big 8. They were hugely popular in Las Vegas, and Elvis Presley was a big fan. He came to see them a number of times and invited them all to a party in his suite. Elvis was complaining that he thought he wasn't a great actor, but Jessie Fagan, one of the dancers with The Big 8, said to him, 'Ah, Elvis, don't be too hard on yourself. Sure, aren't you a great singer?' She eventually married Bill Fuller.

I too saw Paddy on stage in Las Vegas, and across all of Ireland.

Paddy decided to return to Ireland with his wife Helen, to rear their young family. During this time, I had the pleasure of working with him on the *Twink* series and his own show for RTÉ, *Craic'n'Cole*. This was an exceptionally popular series, in which Paddy featured some of his own favourite singers and musicians, interspersed with the man himself making his sax 'talk'. Paddy is a treasure and a pleasure to work with, with a sense of humour that has us laughing all the time.

In 2008, Paddy's *King of the Swingers* album became a bestseller to a legion of followers, spanning all age groups.

As well as his regular stints on stage, Paddy has enjoyed a strong following with his Sunday morning programme on Sunshine Radio, where his relaxed style engages and entertains with music and conversation, all delivered with a healthy potion of humour.

Paddy has been a friend of mine for many, many years and this book delivers a wonderful insight to a true musical legend. I love Paddy (Cosy), a very special man and musician.

John McColgan, October 2020

Chapter 1

Born With a Silver Sax

Some people are said to be born with a silver spoon in their mouths. But it seems as though ace musician and singer Paddy Cole was born with the mouthpiece of a silver saxophone between his lips!

The eight decades that Paddy has spent (so far) on this planet have 'gone by like the blink of an eye', he says. The soundtrack to this musician's life consists not only of the enormously diverse music he plays, but also of the colourful tales he tells. Paddy paints vivid, lived-in word pictures of an ever-changing world. Musically, culturally, economically, environmentally and religiously, the world that Paddy Cole entered over eighty years ago has not always been a cosy place. It has certainly been a chameleon place.

Born on the southern side of the border that divides the Republic of Ireland from Northern Ireland, Paddy even took part in small-time childhood smuggling of goods. During his early school days, he became aware of the tensions and the religious differences in his home area. But he was never partisan to the excesses on either side of that divide.

'We became aware at a certain early age that some boys who we were playing football with around the streets were Protestant lads. They went to one school and we went to the other. I always thought that was unfortunate. But it seemed to be instilled into some children from both sides, and from a young age, that there was a difference between us.'

This was the late 1940s, as the world was slowly recovering from the ashes of the Second World War. Normality was gradually returning, but much more terrifying and tension-filled times were to emerge in the Ireland of the 1950s and the decades that followed. Paddy never allowed religious persuasions or historical sectarianism to play any part in the soundtrack of his life. He has always endeavoured to use music as a unifying force for people of all religious and political persuasions and none.

To begin at the beginning, Santa Claus arrived early at the Cole household in Henry Street, Castleblayney, County Monaghan, in 1939. On 17 December of that year, a bouncing baby boy, subsequently named Paddy, became the second to be born into the family. The family soon moved to Lakeview in the town, and five more siblings were to follow.

Sax playing was in Paddy's DNA, and his dad was probably the first to put the silver sax to the baby's lips. It wasn't long before the little child was secretly climbing onto a table, taking the clarinet from the wall and putting it to his lips himself. But when his father discovered this, for reasons of safety, he moved the instrument out of the youngster's reach to a higher peg on the wall.

Paddy's father, also named Paddy, was a post office worker and also a saxophonist, playing with the local Regal Dance Band and later The Maurice Lynch Orchestra.

His parents were 'great people, who worked so hard to raise a family of seven', says Paddy. 'I often think back about my dad and I admire him a lot for working day and night. He was with the post office, driving a mail van delivering letters and parcels to sub-post offices every morning, as well as being a musician by night.

'There were times when he would only get home from playing, perhaps at a hunt ball or a dance, maybe as far away as Meath, after 3 or 4am. Often, he would not even have time to change out of his dress suit. He would just put on his post office coat over it and away he would go to work. Often he might have to be out again that night, playing at another function.'

Way before Paddy's time, there was a Cole's Number One Band, featuring his father, his uncle Harry and a cousin, Francie Cole. That band played mostly at local dances around Castleblayney. When his father joined the Regal Dance Band, the line-up included 'two or three sax players, sitting down', trumpets and a rhythm section, plus a lady vocalist. 'It was all very formal stuff back then, before he joined The Maurice Lynch Band, who also did some of the new showband stuff. When I was a teenager, we were both playing together in that band.'

It seems that by the time baby Paddy was able to walk and talk – 'and climb' – he was also showing enthusiasm for playing music. And why not, being born into a musical household?

'From an early age, I was aware of my father playing music and of other musicians coming to our house. Instruments were taken out, with musicians comparing saxophones and playing in sessions.'

Memories remain etched in his mind too of how his mother made ends meet while rearing a large family in post-Second World War Ireland. Paddy is still in awe of the sacrifices that she, like so many mothers, had to make back then.

'Times were tough when I was growing up, but we didn't think much about it. Everyone was in similar circumstances, apart, perhaps, from a few families who were merchants or shop owners. Looking back, you would wonder how the mothers of Ireland made ends meet at all.

'My mother was an amazing woman. We shopped in a certain store at the other end of town, where my mother knew the owner. We would go to the shop for groceries as we needed them, and the shopkeeper would mark each purchase down in a book. Then, religiously every Saturday evening, my mother went to the shop and paid for everything that was in the book. A week never went by without my mother paying the bill. Later, when that shop closed, Dan O'Neill, a father of Micky O'Neill who later played drums in my band, had a shop. We would deal there, and it was the same system, with the slate being cleaned every Saturday evening.'

Whenever she could spare a few pounds, his mother would put this away for 'a rainy day' or some special occasion. Paddy has vivid memories of one such instance. This was when, as an aspiring teenage musician, he wanted an expensive mouthpiece for his saxophone.

'I went to Belfast with the bandleader Maurice Lynch to Matchetts Music Store, where he was ordering some instrument. There I saw this new type of mouthpiece that so many players were raving about. But it cost £5, and that was what my father was getting as his week's wages at the time.

'When I came home, I mentioned it, and the next time I was going to the Belfast shop with Maurice, my mother quietly slipped me the £5 note.

Paddy (middle row, fifth from left) at St Mary's National School, Castleblayney, 1949.

Where that £5 came from I will never know. But our parents worked miracles to give whatever they could to their children in those tough times.'

Paddy's mother, Mary Hughes, also from Castleblayney, was also from a musical family. But her people played music of a different genre to the jazz and big band sounds played by his father. 'My mother's people were more into accordion and fiddle playing. While my mother never played an instrument, she was a lovely singer. Both of my parents encouraged music in the family. One of my sisters, Mae, the next in line to me in the family, was a good sax player in her younger years. But there were very few opportunities for girls playing the sax in bands at that time. The only one that I remember doing so was Phyllis Ruane from Ballina in Mayo, who played in the popular Ruanes' band.'

It was a far more equal world for girls in bands decades later, when Paddy toured in places as far away as Jamaica, Las Vegas, New York or New Orleans. Playing in such places never fazed Paddy. And why would it? After all, he was but a child when he started to listen to jazz, big band and Dixieland records. His father would get those old-style 78rpm (revolutions per minute) records by post from America and elsewhere. They were played on a gramophone in the Cole home, and enthusiastically listened to, over and over again.

'We had this wind-up gramophone in a cabinet, three or four feet high. It had a big speaker and there was a great sound off it. My father would send money to cousins of ours in America to get records. Sometimes he would get them from England, or he might occasionally get 78s from other guys who were record collectors.'

Paddy remembers his father sending postal orders to Selmer's shop in London for music-tutor books, as he was self-taught on the saxophone.

Selmer's was an iconic music shop in Charing Cross. It started selling saxophones and other instruments back in 1929. Over the decades it had many famous customers, including ace guitarist Eric Clapton, who bought his first guitar there. Other famous customers who shopped there included members of The Rolling Stones, The Beatles, The Who and Bob Dylan.

'When I think about it now,' says Paddy, 'I am amazed at his dedication, to just keep going, teaching himself how to read and play music from those tutor books. As I got a little older, perhaps when I was about eight or nine, my father would have a tutor left out for me each day before he went to work. I would have to practise on the alto sax after school, and have that piece learned off when he would get home in the evening. At the time I hated it, because I could hear my pals on the street outside playing football.

'Eventually, the more tunes I learned from my father, and the more I listened to the 78s playing on our gramophone, I got to love the music. Firstly, it was the big bands that I liked. But when I heard the New Orleans Dixieland jazz, I thought that was brilliant. I also became friends with others who liked the same sort of records. One was Frank D'Arcy, and another was Vincent McBrierty from Belfast. He became a professor in Trinity College, Dublin, and is still a great buddy of mine.'

Through swapping records with others who had similar tastes in music, he and his pals began learning to play like the musicians they heard on those records.

'Listening to those records, I became a fan of The Original Dixieland Jazz Band and its bandleader Nick LaRocca. You never know what is in store for you in life, because years later, when I brought The Paddy Cole Band to New Orleans, another LaRocca played in my band. We did six or seven tours in New Orleans and on one occasion, when our trumpet player couldn't travel, the guy who deputised for him there was Jimmy LaRocca. He was a son of Nick LaRocca who I used to listen to as a kid on the old gramophone back in Castleblayney.'

Paddy says that in his childhood days, New Orleans was 'a world away', and in his mind's eye, he marvelled at the big-name musicians who played there. He never dreamed that one day, his own name would be up in lights at venues in this great US city, the home of jazz.

'I couldn't believe it when we arrived in New Orleans and saw my name on a poster outside one of the jazz clubs on Bourbon Street. As I had recorded 'Bourbon Street Parade' at that time, I must admit that I was very chuffed. The promoter who took us out there on the tours was a travel agent named Sean Griffin, and we usually had over 100 people going with us on each trip.

'The people in the clubs where we played would say to us after some gigs that it was the best takings they ever had at the bar. But what they did not realise was that there were over 100 extra Irish people there every night. When they would say, "You drew a great crowd of drinking people, Paddy," they didn't know that so many of them were our Irish followers. Of course, we did not make them any the wiser of it either,' laughs Paddy.

While he was full of confidence playing in the top clubs in New Orleans or Las Vegas later in life, it was a shakier start for the teenage Paddy Cole on his first public performance. Indeed, his first tentative steps towards a showbiz career, at the tender age of twelve on a concert stage in his home town, almost ended in disaster.

'I was billed as "Twelve-year-old Paddy Cole, Ireland's youngest saxo-phone player". But I will never forget that night, because I froze when I was supposed to play a solo, before a packed audience in the local Lyric Theatre. My father, who was sitting down, moved over beside me and got the tune started, and then I played on. It was my father's quick action that saved my blushes.'

While he might have suffered from stage fright on his first public performance playing the saxophone, Paddy never lacked confidence when speaking Irish. During his years in both primary and second-level schools in Castleblayney, he got several scholarships and other accolades for his speaking *as Gaeilge*.

'I picked up a love for the Irish language at primary school. My father would speak a *cúpla focail* at home, but it was just a subject that I got to love at school. There were many other subjects that I found far more difficult, but I always got unbelievable marks for Irish. I remember getting two summer scholarships, for six weeks each time, for the Ranafast Gaeltacht in Donegal. Then came the year when I was so excited about making it three in a row. However, my parents did not share my excitement that summer.

'I remember running home to tell them I had got the three in a row to go to the Gaeltacht that year. But my father looked up from the newspaper he was reading and said, "You can forget about it this year. I've got you a summer job at Isaac Haillis garage, filling petrol." So I couldn't go that summer, because the few quid I could earn was far more important.'

Paddy has never lost his love for the Irish language. He still likes to speak a few words *as Gaeilge*, including on his radio programme on Sunday mornings on Sunshine Radio (106.8 FM) in Dublin.

'It's only a wee bit of the language that I use from time to time. When you are not speaking it regularly, you lose the *blas* for it. If I were in a Gaeltacht area and the locals were talking in Irish, they would be doing it effortlessly and so quickly, I wouldn't be able to keep up. But my wife Helen is a fluent Irish speaker, and all our four grandchildren went to the Gaelscoil here in Dublin. They are all fluent Irish speakers,' he adds with a hint of a grandparent's quiet pride in his voice.

So, the third generation of Coles have a flair for the Irish language just like their grandfather. Paddy first realised that he had a talent for it in his early schooldays, being taught by the nuns in Castleblayney. Indeed, when the Bishop of Clogher came to officially open a new boys' primary school in the town, Paddy was selected to read the address of welcome in Irish. He says he learned every word of it 'off by heart'.

When he moved on to the Vocational School in the town, his love of the *Gaeilge* continued. When he had to rush off to play with The Maurice Lynch Band following an Irish exam, Paddy was so proficient with the language that he completed a two-hour examination in a little over twenty minutes.

'Maurice Lynch's band wagon was parked discreetly about twenty or thirty yards up the road, to collect me from the school. Obviously, the teacher spied it there. I was running down the stairs after completing the paper in twenty minutes when the headmaster, Master Murray, who was a lovely person, saw me rushing off. He said, "Cole, are you ill?" I replied that I was not, but that I had finished the exam. He thought I had only completed part of the exam, and his stern response was that he would be "watching with interest" what my results would be.

'Almost unbelievably, I got something like ninety-five per cent in that exam. I am not saying that I was a genius at school at all – there were other subjects that stumped me completely. But the Irish seemed to come naturally to me, and I loved it.'

The young Paddy Cole reads a welcome in Irish to the Bishop at the opening of the new school in Castleblayney, 1950s.

The Maurice Lynch Band, 1956/7.
Back: Paddy Cole jnr, Peter Hickey;
Third row: John Beatty, Frankie Lynch, Mickey O'Neill;
Second row: Maurice Lynch, Gerry Muldoon, Audie Heaney;
Front: Paddy Cole snr.

There was singing to be done at school too. 'When it came to Christmas time, I was always asked to take part in carol singing as a youngster. They used to think I was a good singer. But often, when announcing a song on stage, I say that "I'm not a great singer, and I've got the records to prove it."

'There was also a marching band in Castleblayney that some of my mother's brothers were in. They were called The Waveney, and when they would be going out to march around town, perhaps with a winning local team, they always called on me to join them. I would arrive out with the saxophone, and I loved the bit of craic doing that.'

Young Paddy became a childhood small-time smuggler too, across the border between the Irish Republic and Northern Ireland. But it was in a fun sort of way, and he looks back on it with amusement.

'We used to go across the border to Crossmaglen. On the first part of the trip, we'd get the train to Culloville, which is a little village a few miles from Castleblayney. We'd get off the train on the Republic side and walk across the border to Crossmaglen. The two items we would usually smuggle were white loaf bread, because evidently the bread in the South wasn't great at that time, and sometimes paraffin oil, which I presume was also scarce in the South. We'd buy something like six loaves of white bread, a gallon of paraffin oil and sometimes butter. It was all small-time stuff.

'Walking back to the southern side, we'd have the bread all well wrapped, up and the paraffin oil tightly sealed in a can. That was in case we had to throw the lot over a hedge or a ditch if we saw the customs men patrolling the roads. After they had gone past, we'd go back and lift the goods out from the ditch or the hedge. Then we'd walk back and board the train home to Castleblayney,' laughs Paddy.

Ironically, the house where the Coles lived was located across the road from a border customs depot. Sometimes, 'if big-time smugglers were caught', the family would know it first.

'Sometimes we would awaken at five in the morning to the sound of a lorry load of pigs squealing in the customs yard across from our house. We'd know immediately that some of the big boys in a smuggling ring had been caught. Later, the customs officials would drive away with the lorry to Dundalk or some other place for further examination and disposal,' says Paddy.

One 'alleged' big time smuggler was accosted by customs officials outside a pub in Muckno Street, Castleblayney, but the evidence melted away right in front of the officials' eyes. 'The customs officials obviously saw that the man's car, parked outside the pub, was sitting well down on the springs. They suspected he was carrying a big load of stuff that he might have smuggled across the border.

'They went up to him in the pub and asked him to hand over the keys of his car, so they could take it to the Garda station. He replied that he would do so, but he needed to take something out of the glove compartment first.

'They allowed him to sit into the car, whereupon he pressed a button, which it seems set off some sort of device that set the car, with its load of butter, on fire. There was panic, and people running hither and thither, as flames from the vehicle leaped into the air and the burning butter started flowing away down the street. So, there was no evidence, and the "alleged" smuggler got away with it because the evidence had melted.'

While Paddy and his pals often played barefoot in the street around Castleblayney, he never had to go barefoot to school, unlike some other boys from the country. Years later, when he told his own children that he had walked barefoot to school, his mother was less than impressed. 'The

The last train from Castleblayney, 15 October 1957. Can you spot Paddy?

children told my mother, Lord have mercy on her, that I was telling them stories about going to school barefoot. She immediately whipped out a photograph of me going to school wearing a pair of beautiful brown shoes. That settled that, and we had many a laugh about it afterwards.'

Ireland of the 1940s and 1950s was an economically stagnant country. But Paddy says that he never noticed, as everybody seemed to be 'in the same boat'. He says that his was an idyllic childhood in many ways.

'Looking back, we had a fantastic time, with lots of simple pastimes and hobbies. We were lucky to have the beautiful scenery around Castleblayney, with Hope Castle and the lake where we fished. We would often go over there to play on the Black Island. We crossed over an old drawbridge to get there so that we could walk and play around the island.'

Those are happy memories, but he admits that corporal punishment, which does not fall into the same joyful category, was 'more or less' accepted in schools in those times. 'If you did something wrong in class, or if you were late for school, you got "three of the best" [slaps with a cane] on both hands. That was the punishment, no matter how cold the morning was. Looking back on it now, it was a terrible thing to have to face any morning, but even more so on cold winter mornings.'

Paddy's mother often warned him and his siblings about the dangers of the TB (tuberculosis) epidemic in Ireland when they were going to school in 1947-50. 'I was only a child of eight or nine years back then, but I have vague memories of my mother warning us to stay away from other kids who had been in the sanatorium for TB. We had to stay away from them, and they had to remain quarantined themselves. It was a bit like the Covid-19 virus of 2020. People were very wary of TB back then, and of even exchanging books or newspapers with those who had TB. There were all sorts of theories doing the rounds that TB travelled on books, papers and magazines and other strange ways. Many were afraid of their lives of contracting it via such strange sources. But like all such epidemics, it passed, and please God the Covid-19 will pass too. However, in my mother's day, Lord have mercy on her, if someone said TB could be controlled and eradicated, they would not believe you. But thank God, it was sorted out medically, and hopefully so also will Covid-19 be,' says Paddy.

Minister Dr Noel Browne, having himself recovered from TB at a sanatorium in the UK, led the fight against the ravages of the disease in Ireland. He introduced free screening for all suspected of having TB, and built specialised hospitals and sanitoria. That, and the development of a new vaccine, rid Ireland of the scourge of TB. But Dr Browne became embroiled in a separate conflict with the Catholic Church, which controlled most hospitals then, regarding a free healthcare scheme for mothers and children. He subsequently resigned as a Minister.

Schools in southern Ireland were mostly operated by the Catholic Church back then. But the corporal punishment meted out both by lay and religious teachers does not seem to have damaged or dimmed his faith. Paddy says his religious faith, and that of his wife Helen, has always been important to them. He says that faith and going to Church regularly and taking their children there was always important when rearing their family. That included even the years living in different circumstances in a place sometimes called 'sin city, USA' – Las Vegas.

Some of his most vivid memories of childhood are of the family on their knees praying the Rosary, 'and the trimmings, which were twice as long'. His mother would lead them in their prayers every night. 'My mother would pray for everyone – cousins in America, and other cousins here, there and everywhere. There might also be prayers for people who were sick, or even for a woman whose hens were not laying – everything was prayed for,' he laughs.

They sometimes prayed for their teachers too, including those who doled out the slaps. Paddy notes that not all their teachers dished out this punishment. 'We had some great teachers too, and some of them taught us four-part harmonies when we were preparing for concerts. That was even in national school. There was a Master O'Toole, who was brilliant. He was teaching young fellows such as us four-part harmonies on intricate pieces of music. I can still remember those pieces of music, right up to this present time.'

As the 1940s morphed into the fifties, sixties and seventies, Paddy moved up the ladder to the top. The big time brought its joys, romance, TV and radio appearances and stage successes, plus world-wide travel. Meanwhile in his homeland, there were some sad and tension-filled times, and the music and dancing scene didn't get through it unscathed either.

Chapter 2

Sleeping Like Spoons in Scotland

Sing me a song of a lad that is gone,

Say, could that lad be I?

Merry of soul he sailed on a day

Over the sea to Skye.

Robert Louis Stevenson (1892)

The Gorbals was a tough area of Glasgow, which is long gone now. It consisted mostly of blocks of tenement flats, and it was Glasgow Celtic Territory. Paddy (Pat) Crerand was born in the heart of The Gorbals and was a hero to the people there as he starred for Celtic Soccer Club back then. He later played for Man United and is currently with Manchester United TV.

'Luckily for our safety, Paddy Crerand became very friendly with the band when we first played Glasgow. I'm still great friends with him today and we have gone on holidays with him on occasion,' says Paddy Cole.

The streets around the Earl Street ballroom, when the teenage Paddy Cole first played there with The Maurice Lynch Band, seemed like something out of a Wild West film. Obviously, befriending Paddy Crerand, who was the same age as Paddy Cole, was a safety net for the young sax player and his band colleagues.

'Everybody respected Paddy Crerand, because The Gorbals was Celtic country. He was a hero there. Paddy would walk through the streets with us after the gig to the end of The Gorbals, where we would get a taxi back to our band wagon.

'It was exciting for me going on that first trip to play in Glasgow – my first time playing outside Ireland. It was brilliant to become a lifelong friend with Paddy Crerand too. He had a lot of relations in Donegal, and a lot of Donegal emigrants would attend our dances in Glasgow, as would emigrants from other places. Some of them were prone to fighting a bit at the dances. If the slightest little thing irritated the wrong person, the row was on!

'Don't get me wrong – we have great memories of playing there, and there were lots of people also at the dances from my home county of Monaghan. At weekends, some other Irish emigrants, who were tunnelling in the north of Scotland, would come down to Glasgow to visit relations and go to the dance. Jesus! All hell could break out at times. I often said afterwards that the Coles were great runners any time there was trouble.'

From childhood, Paddy Cole was a Glasgow Celtic fan, but, he hastens to add, not for any political or religious reasons. 'I was always a Celtic fan

First trip to Glasgow: Paddy, Michael O'Byrne, Mickey O'Neill
and Paddy senior.

because an uncle of mine, Tim Hughes, lived in Glasgow and was a big Celtic supporter. He would come home to visit in the summer when I was a kid, and all the talk would be about this famous team followed by many Irish in Scotland. I started following Celtic at that stage, but I would never be involved in the politics of it. However, I was made aware at that time of Glasgow Rangers not playing Catholic footballers.'

Paddy Crerand had a distinguished soccer career, starting in 1957 at Glasgow Celtic. Even if tinged with controversy for his steeliness on the field at times, he was capped on sixteen occasions with Scotland. He played with Manchester United from 1963, and went on to win the European Cup with the team in 1968. 'We were Manchester United fans as well, and of course I was thrilled to bits when Paddy Crerand joined United. My two sons, Pearse and Pat, are United fans also.'

Years later, Paddy was delighted to be present with his two sons when Manchester United had a famous win. 'We went over to many of their matches, but we keep remembering one particular time, when United were hosting Liverpool and they beat them. Oh boy! There was some big celebration that night. We stayed over in Manchester, and went along to a jazz club operated by Don Long, who had played with me in The Capitol Showband. I put a clarinet in my travel bag going to that match, and went on stage and played that night at the celebrations in Don's club.'

That was decades after Paddy first toured in Scotland, crammed with six others and the band's equipment into a Commer van. They were told by the driver to 'sleep like spoons' when travelling through the rocky roads around the Highlands. In the middle of the tour, they also had to cross the tumbling seas to Stornoway.

Paddy, Frankie Lynch (drums) and Audie Heaney (singer) on the way to the island of Stornoway with The Maurice Lynch Band, 1957/8.

The boys from 'Blayney braved the crosswinds and the tidal streams, sometimes flowing from two directions, in the Minch sea strait. The translation of its name from Scots Gaelic is 'the tiring or wearisome sea'. The band loved reaching the relative tranquillity of Stornoway – but it sure was a long way to go to play!

'After playing Glasgow, we went to halls in Edinburgh and on Oban, Thurso and Wick, and then over the sea to Stornoway.' Nowadays people can fly to Stornoway from four airports in the UK. But when Paddy Cole was going there as a teenager, it was much more difficult to get there and back.

'The ballroom in Stornoway would be packed to capacity and the people were all Scots Gaelic speakers. It is very much like our Irish, and I could converse a little bit with them because of my own love for the *Gaeilge* at school. They were lovely people. We would go there from the mainland by boat for one night only, and come back the next day, also by boat.

'The promoter Bill Fehily owned a ballroom in Wick and another one in Thurso, and he would sell on our show to other promoters, such as on Stornoway. Afterwards we would start travelling down to England. That was one hell of a journey. "Sleep like spoons, and when one man turns, make sure you all turn the same way." So roared our band leader Maurice Lynch over the noisy engine of the van. He would shout, "All turn!" and we were all obliged to turn the same way at the same time. We never worried in the slightest about things like that in those times. We were young and it was so exciting. All we wanted to do was to get to the next venue, to go on the stage and play music.'

Paddy says his experience as a teenager playing in Scotland was a great grounding for him years later, regarding the type of programme an Irish band should play in Las Vegas. 'Maurice was a great showman, a great entertainer, who played trumpet as well as piano accordion. He and a guy called Tommy Toal, the main vocalist, knew hundreds of songs. When Maurice strapped on that accordion, it was almost a competition between the two of them for who could sing the most songs.

'Dancing at that time could be from 9pm to 2am, or even 9pm to 3am, and it was hard on the lips for a sax player. But it was demanding for everybody in all the bands at that time, as there were no support acts.

'We were doing a cross section of everything – a variety of music to suit all tastes. In Maurice's band we were playing skiffle, the Bill Haley 'Rock Around the Clock' stuff, also Irish and Scottish tunes and ballads. We did Al Jolson medleys and, sitting down behind the music stands, we did the big band stuff such as Glen Miller material as well.

'Years later, I remember when playing with The Big 8 in Las Vegas that having a variety of music was the key to success. At that time, you might have a country band in one club and they only played country, a Dixieland jazz band playing all Dixieland, and so on. Even in Vegas – vastly different, yet in some ways similar to Stornoway – we would play a bit of everything and the places would be packed. The late Tom Dunphy would sing country, Brendan Bowyer would do his rock'n'roll, Twink did the ladies' songs and we did some Dixieland jazz. We also had a fifteen-minute spot in the middle where we had Irish dancers on stage. I played the tin whistle and they came on and danced Irish jigs and reels.'

Speaking on RTÉ radio's *Des's Island Discs* in March 2020, Paddy gave credit to his friends in a rival showband, The Royal, for introducing this trend to Las Vegas first. 'It was unique when The Royal Showband did a very varied programme the first time they went to play in Las Vegas, some years before The Big 8 did likewise.'

On his first trip to Scotland, Paddy felt more confident because his father, Paddy Snr, was also in the band. It was also a great bonding experience for both father and son to be working and travelling together. 'My father would help Maurice Lynch a lot, because apart from being bandleader, Maurice was also the driver. My dad would give him a break from driving from time to time, as would some other band members.

'We had great times together, my father and myself. We would go for walks together during the days, looking up historical sites in small towns in the north of Scotland. Sometimes we would go to local libraries and museums, because both of us were interested in all that sort of stuff. It was so supportive for me to have my dad there, if I needed any advice regarding any issues with the sax. He was a great man to go to if I had any problem with a reed, if it needed repairing, or anything like that.'

Paddy is evasive in his answer about his dad being around when young Scottish girls might be taking an interest in his teenage son. 'He didn't take much notice of that, and it was all innocent stuff anyway, just up chatting to girls after dances. Like many other young musicians then, I probably thought that I was a Casanova. They would get some shock if they saw me now,' he laughs.

Before his international debut in Scotland, and before becoming a regular member of The Maurice Lynch Band, Paddy says that 'at thirteen or fourteen', he and two others had a skiffle group. 'I was playing a bit of guitar in the skiffle group, and I was brutally bad. We were singing all the Lonnie Donegan songs that were hits then, and we just lived for the next gig.

'We must've been a bit ambitious when we called ourselves The Jazz Group. We just had a drummer, Kevin McKenna, his cousin Sally McKenna, who played the accordion, and I was on saxophone and vocals. We were young teenagers, and we would travel out to small halls such as the one in Oram and play from 9pm to 2am. The lights in the halls were Tilley lamps, as there was no rural electrification then.'

The Tilley lamp got its name from John Tilley, the man who invented it in the early 1800s. It had a pressurised tank filled with kerosene. As the fuel was forced into the lamp's chamber, it vaporised, producing a very bright light. The arrival of rural electrification in Ireland in the 1950s quickly made this form of lighting redundant in dance halls. But in those years, Paddy remembers the person in charge of each hall pumping up the Tilley lamps before the band started playing.

Paddy and the other two teenage musicians had to pay for the power they used on stage. 'We had to pay the guy that drove us out to the hall an extra fee for also using his car battery to power our amplification. He would charge an additional five shillings for the use of the battery for that purpose. Our fee was £5, and when we paid for the hire of the car and the use of the battery, we were lucky to have £1 each.

'One day in town, I brazenly went to the man who organised the dance in Oram hall and asked if he could put our fee up to £6. He said he would have to put this to the hall committee. They came back, saying they agreed to our fee being increased by £1, and I thought that was great. But there was a catch – instead of us playing from nine to two, the dance now had to go on until 3am. We didn't mind – the extra £1 between the three of us was good, because we were only thirteen or fourteen at the time. Perhaps if we were financially more forward-thinking, we might have got extra money by looking for a sixty per cent share of the takings.'

Paddy quickly gave up playing football during school days after discovering, to his cost, that it did not always mix with playing music. 'There was a boy with me at school named John Coleman, who was a very rough football player. He was a lovely fellow and a great friend of mine. But as soon as he put on the football boots or a jersey it was like going to the Korean War!

'We were playing against his team one day and he gave me a box in the mouth – accidently I believe. My lip went way up during the match, just hours before I was due to play in a small hall in a place called Latton. I was unable to play due to my swollen lip, and I missed out on the ten shillings I would have been paid. That was a fortune in those days, and so I immediately took the decision to end my footballing career.'

With his usual joviality, Paddy adds that he doesn't think that his team, the Castleblayney Faughs, were too concerned about him quitting. If he had continued playing, he might have got to mark another midfield player on the opposing Oram team, his friend and fellow musician Big Tom McBride.

'I knew Tom very well and as I was a midfield player, that could have been a bruising encounter if myself and Tom clashed. Tom was a great footballer; he had the height and the big build, and he could be teak-tough too. As I said on the tribute night for him on RTÉ TV, he was always known as a gentle giant. But he was not so gentle if you were marking him at midfield.'

While Paddy had some interest in playing football during the 1950s, those years were also exciting times to be involved in music. 'The whole music scene was changing in Ireland at that time. Loads of people were listening to foreign radio stations and collecting records of this new type of music that was coming, and we were all part of it.'

These were the years after the Korean War, and Paddy and his friends were vaguely aware of that conflict. 'Like most people, we would be listening

With Big Tom and Rose, and Helen, as Paddy and Tom
receive the Freedom of Castleblayney.

to news reports and reading the papers and sadly hearing about the number of young men losing their lives. Unfortunately, as life moved on, many of those people were quickly forgotten. Probably like some of today's younger generation not knowing much about the Gulf War or the Vietnam War, we as Irish teenagers of the 50s, did not know much about The Korean War either. It is sad how so many people lost their lives in wars, including in our own country.'

Paddy says he always tried not to be bitter about things that happened in Northern Ireland, and he always looked at music as a unifying force for all. 'When we played in the bands, we were never bothered about who was Protestant or Catholic. Genuinely, I would not know or care what religion, if any, those who played with me in bands were. Neither were we bothered about what religious persuasion those who danced to our music were. We just tried to walk a middle line and accept that there are lovely people on both sides, and bad people on each side also.'

But as Paddy is from the border area, and the bands he played in did a lot of Northern Ireland gigs, he remembers cross-border travel restrictions from his early days. 'When we would cross the border to play in the North, we had to have a sheet that listed all the instruments and equipment we had. The Southern customs officials would check it first, and then the Northern customs officials would also check it.

'We also had to put in a request to them, stating what time the band would be coming back across the border. For example, if we were playing in Armagh and the dance was over at 1am, we would have a request in for crossing at the Keady customs post by 2.30am. If we were late arriving back – if it was 2.40am – we couldn't legally get back across the border. So it was important to request a time for crossing the border that gave a bit of leeway.

If not, we might be sleeping in the band wagon until morning. It was more difficult to gauge what time we would be crossing the border if we were playing further up north in Antrim. But we just had to get accustomed to working with those border restrictions from the 1950s onwards.'

Meanwhile, over in the USA in the 1950s, Elvis Presley and others had taken the music scene by storm. Rock'n'roll music quickly arrived on this side of the Atlantic Ocean too. The music stands were pushed aside, and musicians no longer sat down, but moved around the stage. The 'show' part of the performance now became more important for the bands – and the showbands were born.

'The Clipper Carlton from Strabane are credited with being the first showband.' So states Paddy in an interview with Sean Creedon in *Ireland's Own* magazine, 24 April 2020. And The Maurice Lynch Band were not far behind The Clippers (as they were also called) in putting the show into their programme.

'I will never forget the first time that I saw The Clipper Carlton in the ballroom in Castleblayney,' says Paddy. 'I was fascinated by them. They were in light blue suits at a time when we mostly wore dress suits and dickie bows on stage. They looked American, with their crew cut hairstyles and the light blue suits. They stood up and they played all those hits by the big American stars of that era, such as Bill Haley and Johnny Ray.

'So, after seeing The Clippers, we decided to start doing all those sorts of songs, and we loved it. The Clipper Carlton did lead the way for us all in that change on the Irish dance scene. Maurice was quick to spot that this was going to be a new trend in entertainment. Then we started to get rid of the music stands for part of our performances. We'd take a break and go into the dressing room and change our jackets. When we came back out,

The Clipper Carlton, the first band to put the 'show' into 'showband'.

we had discarded the dicky bows and were wearing light-coloured jackets as well as the black pants. The crowd would gather up around the stage when we put on a bit of a show – thus becoming a showband.'

Around that time, Paddy realised that music was going to be his life, but he says it was not a conscious decision on his part. 'I always figured that whatever I would do would be in music. Even before going into it full-time, I was busy with The Maurice Lynch Band, sometimes playing five nights a week and going as far away as Dublin and Waterford for gigs.'

At that time, there was no such thing as a motorway in the country, and a journey from Monaghan to Waterford or Dublin or Galway was very tiring for six musicians crammed into a van. 'The journey to Waterford, for the first time, seemed unbelievably long to me as a youngster in the band. The roads were bad and slow for travelling on. When we got to Dublin, we stopped for a snack of some sort. It was at a place called Molly's in Richmond Street, which remained a famous stop-off venue and meeting place for musicians during the showband era.

'From there we would hit the road for Waterford, and we were lucky that it was an early dance, from 8 to 11pm. We were back into the wagon by midnight and on our way back to Dublin. We would stop off at Molly's again for another snack before heading back to Castleblayney. It seemed like a marathon trip for us to go to Waterford.

'But it was much worse for bands based in Derry or north Donegal. Just imagine the length of journeys those bands had to make to dances in Cork, Killarney or Dingle, travelling on terrible bad roads. Those musicians spent most of their time in band wagons, and you can understand why so many bands split up. There were sure to be tensions when fellows were travelling, sitting in close proximity to each other, night after night. They were also rehearsing together, having meals together, playing on stage together, and travelling to and from the gigs together. They were bound to get on each other's nerves, and sometimes something just had to give. It was tougher than for us, "sleeping like spoons" on our occasional trips through Scotland and down to London.'

Just like playing for the Irish emigrants in Glasgow, even in the often-rowdy dancehall in The Gorbals, Paddy says he always loved playing for the Irish in London. 'A lot of guys and girls that I had gone to school with would see it advertised in the Irish newspapers in England that The Maurice Lynch Band was coming to London. They would travel in large numbers to see us in Cricklewood or Fulham Broadway or The Blarney on Tottenham Court Road or The Banba. The Monaghan crowd that had emigrated to London would be there in their hundreds at those dances. It was great to meet up with those school pals and chat with them after the dances. There was always also the benefit of a resident band playing support in those places.

'One such ballroom, The Gresham on Holloway Road, was a palatial place. It was a fabulous venue to play in, and it was owned by a fellow from outside Castleblayney named Tommie Gorman. It had the first revolving bandstand we had ever seen. The resident band would go around and then we would go around.

'On an occasional night, it would malfunction and it might have to be pushed around. But usually we just sailed around on it while playing. It was a big thrill for us to play on a revolving stage in London back then. While I won't mention names, I remember one musician in the business asking if we liked played on "the revolting stage" in The Gresham.

'When I think back to those times, they were happy days and nights. If there was stress in our lifestyle and if it seemed like hard work, we realised that a lot of people worked harder than us. Those included especially the emigrants working on roads and building sites. Times were tough in most jobs back then, and we were lucky to love what we were doing. I wouldn't change those memories of my early days as a musician for anything,' says Paddy with more than a hint of nostalgia in his voice.

Chapter 3

A Garda, a Butcher or a Sparky

P addy's proficiency in the Irish language, along with his height of six feet, did not go unnoticed by the local chief of the Gardaí. 'The local Garda sergeant suggested that as I was fluent in Irish, a requirement to join the police force in Ireland at that time, I could have a successful career as a Garda. I believe that my parents were in favour of me doing so, as my father tried to encourage me in that direction. He said that perhaps I could continue playing by becoming a member of the Garda Band,' says Paddy, who wasn't interested in becoming one of the boys in blue.

Taking a year off school, Paddy explored a couple of other job opportunities, including as part of the rural electrification scheme of the time.

'A local businessman, Willie McCauley, who had an electrical shop, got the contract to "wire", as they called it, a lot of the houses in country areas. Another man named Jackie Doherty was the real electrician, and I was sort of serving my time with him. For some of the houses that I helped to wire, 'tis amazing that some of the creatures who lived in them survived afterwards!

'I was often going into houses still half asleep, after playing the night before in Armagh and getting home at four in the morning. When I look back on it, sure it was as dangerous for the people in the houses as for myself.'

In the 1995 book by Tim Ryan *Tell Roy Rogers I'm Not In* (Blackwater Press), Paddy recalls an incident when wiring a dairy. It sounds humorous, but he could have been killed: 'Jackie Doherty told me to put in a fuse to test the current. I walked back to my job and foolishly grabbed the ends of the two wires I was working on. The next thing I remember was waking up on the far side of the dairy among a heap of milk cans. If I had stuck to it, I would be stone dead.'

Paddy recalls the awe of people when the new electric light was switched on. Frightened spiders would be scurrying for cover into boltholes as they were blinded by this new brightness. 'People would be running around with brooms and dusters, clearing cobwebs out of corners and cleaning dust off the tops of cabinets. Some people embraced the new electric current coming into their homes, but others were afraid of it, which is understandable too. Here we were, digging channels down the sides of the walls in their kitchens and burying wires in wooden casings into those walls. Some people insisted on being able to see it outside the surface of the walls, and so we had to just attach the casing to the walls. But the walls weren't very solid – a lot of them were just stones covered with loose plaster. So it was a tough job to attach the casings to some of them.

'In one home, where we spent all day chiselling out channels for inserting casings into the walls, when we came back the next day, the owner had tried to finish the job himself. He buried the wires, without any casings, and we had to take them all out again. But the householders looked after us extremely well. They would usually cook a lunch for us, and we might take a snack with us from home as well. It was interesting moving the gear from one house to the next. The ESB [Electricity Supply Board] workers came along after us and wired those houses up to the mains.'

But working as an electrician wasn't the career path that Paddy wanted, and he didn't make the cut either as a butcher! However, he says he had fun times in that job, and became a champion sausage maker. But other aspects, such as slaughtering animals, are not his favourite memories.

'When I took a year out from school, I was doing what might be termed an apprenticeship to the butchery business. It was with Mallon's butchers, and mostly what I did was deliver meat around the town to people, riding around on a bicycle with a big basket on the front of it. But I also witnessed the slaughtering in the yard, which was a tough experience for a youngster. When I think about it now, I probably would not be able to witness it. But I have to say that Jimmy Mallon did it in the most humane way possible, and everything was done according to the rules. The inspectors came regularly, and the guys adhered to the most rigorous of regulations.

'What I was good at was making sausages. They taught me how to do all that, and I was proud as punch going home and saying that I made so many pounds of sausages today. It was interesting work, as I liked being outside and I spent most of my time whistling while cycling around delivering the meat. Also, as Kevin McKenna, the drummer in the little jazz group we had, worked in a grocery shop a few doors down, we regularly exchanged music ideas. They were happy times, and the Mallon family were lovely people to work for. As soon as the next year of second-level school came around, I was sent back to the books. But to this day, Frank Mallon, now one of the biggest meat processors in Ireland, is a good friend. I often talk to him about the times that I worked for his father and his uncle Eamon, and how lovely they were to work for.'

Paddy could also have gone to work in the office of a local furniture factory, but he passed up this opportunity too. 'It was the McElroy furniture factory, operated by brothers Gussie and Eddie, and they came to the school looking for somebody to work in the office. I was suggested by Master Murray, but I turned it down, for two reasons. Firstly, the wages to serve your time in the office were ten shillings (fifty cent) per week. But I was getting that for one night playing with The Maurice Lynch Band, and I was doing that five nights a week. Also, as a lot of my pals were working on the factory floor making furniture, I would have preferred to work with them rather than in the office. But it was nice of them to make the offer of the office job.

'A few of the boys that worked in McElroy's furniture factory were also part-time musicians at that time. Some of them went into the music business full-time later. They included Ronnie Duffy, who became the drummer with Big Tom and the Mainliners, and Seamus McMahon (RIP), who was lead guitar player in the band. Another was a man named Frank Gormley, who played in The Regal Dance Orchestra with my father, and I'm sure there are others.'

Ronnie Duffy married Paddy's sister Carmel Cole and when the Mainliners and Big Tom parted company for a while, Ronnie became the

The Regal Dance Orchestra, Castleblayney, 1947. Front: Sean Farrell, Paddy Cole snr, Frank Gormley, Frank McArdle, Christine McManus, Sadie Loughman; back: Jack McManus, Phil Farrell, Pat Donaghue.

drummer in The Paddy Cole band. 'Ronnie was an integral part of the "magic beat" associated with Big Tom's band, as was Seamus McMahon, and another school friend of mine – John Beattie on organ. When we were young lads in the fifties, John was practising the piano and I would go up to his house with the sax after school some days. The two of us would play music in the afternoon in the sitting room. He had a beautiful piano in the house and was a lovely guy, as he still is. He was always a great musician, and he had that unique sound.

'All the other lads in Big Tom's band were local too. Trombone player the late Cyril McKevitt was another school pal of mine. He used to cycle in from the country to our school. Then you had Ginger Morgan, the original lead singer, on bass, and Henry McMahon on the sax. Big Tom originally played the baritone sax as well as singing. He was such a big guy, even when young, that the baritone sax looked like an alto sax when he lifted it.'

As well as playing music, some of these boys were learning woodwork and metalwork at the vocational school. 'The principal, Mr Murray, also taught woodwork, while a Mr Phil Giblin from Sligo taught metalwork. They were great teachers, as was Mr Hanratty, who taught us rural science. Even yet I can remember him saying, if you are planting something it's best to do so any month with an "R" in it. These are little things about gardening that my wife still cannot understand how I got to know about. We had a great Irish teacher called Mr Markey. He was a tough man, who took foot-ball very seriously, more so than I did.'

Instead of mastering playing football, Paddy was playing two of the most difficult instruments to master, the clarinet and the sax. The former is the more difficult of the two, he says. 'I learned to play the instruments the wrong way around. If you learn the clarinet first, the sax will come relatively easy to you. But as I did it the opposite way, it was much harder for me to learn the clarinet. There is a different type of fingering for it, as you must cover the holes with your fingers, while there are pads on the saxophone. Neither instrument was one that most young people would be learning to play at that time. People in our area going to music lessons were learning piano or guitar or violin, or maybe a concert flute. But as my father was a sax player, and there were a few others also in The Regal Dance Orchestra, it was like second nature for me to learn the sax.'

On the *Late Late Show*, Gay Byrne (RIP) once described Paddy Cole as 'one of the greatest jazzers in the business'. After Gay's death, Paddy was one of the artists selected to play on the tribute TV show in 2019 in memory of the iconic TV and radio presenter. On that programme, Paddy played the tune that is perhaps most associated with him, 'King of the Swingers'.

The audio clip of Gay saying that Paddy was a top 'jazzer' was also used in another RTÉ programme in 2011, *A Little Bit Showband*. Paddy Cole was interviewed on that programme, and elaborated on why he chose to play sax and clarinet instead of other instruments.

'My dad was one of the first men to bring a saxophone to Castleblayney. We grew up listening to records that he got sent from America – the big bands, Count Basie, Duke Ellington, all of those. That was how I also got listening to traditional Dixieland jazz. That type of New Orleans jazz caught my imagination. As soon as I heard that, I wanted to play it.'

Paddy admired the playing of several well-known saxophone and clarinet players as a youngster. Some were popular players from the Irish scene, while one was lesser known on this side of the Atlantic, but a star in the home of jazz, New Orleans. His name was Sam Butera, and he played with the famous bandleader Louis Prima, also from New Orleans.

'I always liked Sam Butera's style. In Ireland, I admired the saxophone playing of Gay McIntyre from Derry. There was a guy in Dublin named John Curran who was a lovely sax player that I also admired. Dublin also had a family of sax players, the McGuinness family – Rory and Johnny were two of those who were great players also. People that I worked with during the showband era included Jim Farley, who was a fine player of both sax and clarinet. Trumpeters Paul Sweeney and Bram McCarthy, who played with me in The Capitol, were great brass players, as was Don Long on trombone.

'For the foreign influences, I'd have to say that Acker Bilk was a real big influence on me. He was a brilliant clarinet player, who had a fabulous tone. One compliment I can pay to him is that when we heard him on the radio in New York, the presenter said, "It says on the record sleeve a clarinet, but it must be a soprano sax." That was a real compliment to the lovely fat sound that Acker Bilk was getting on the clarinet.'

Acker Bilk, who died in 2014, is best known for his composition 'Stranger on the Shore', which spent a staggering fifty-five weeks in the UK pop charts in 1961. While he failed to unseat Cliff Richard's 'The Young Ones' from the top of the charts in his homeland, Acker Bilk had a number one with it in America. The tune has been covered by countless artists over the years.

Paddy says he would listen to records by other artists at home, but once he was playing with The Maurice Lynch Band, he had few opportunities to see other bands live.

'I liked The Johnny Flynn Band from Tuam, with drummer Frankie Hannon doing all the Fats Domino numbers. He had a great way with him, and had a great style on the drums. He sang "Blueberry Hill",

Greeting the great Acker Bilk at Dublin Airport.

which I tried to sing later with The Capitol. Johnny Flynn's band were extremely popular around the North of Ireland in the fifties and sixties.

'Johnny Quigley from Derry also had a fabulous band. They did a show similar to what we were doing in Maurice's band. They would sit at the music stands and play orchestrations for the first part of the show. Then they would go in and change. They would come out in gold lamé jackets and strut their stuff for the second half. Johnny and his brothers Mike and Joe were all great musicians. Of course, we all admired The Clipper Carlton, and The Dixies from Cork were another talented band.

'As we were playing the same nights that the other bands were playing, it was always hard to get a night off to see other bands play. It's a bit like years later, when we were playing at the Cork Jazz Festival, which I did for over thirty years, people would ask, did you hear such-and-such a player? But we heard nobody else, because we were playing at the same times that they were playing.

'It was the same during the showband years, but when we did get a chance, we went to see our favourite bands play. I remember the excitement of going to see The Royal Showband in the City Hall in Armagh, and by God they were an exciting band. I can still see Eddie Sullivan blowing that trumpet, and he was such a strong trumpet player. I admired that band so much. They covered a great cross section of the music that was popular at that time. You could see why they had such a huge following and became the most popular of all the showbands. The crowd went wild for them that night in Armagh.

'Brendan Bowyer was dynamic on stage. I was so impressed with him doing the Elvis Presley stuff, but also with his big ballad singing. He sang one that night that always stands out in my memory. He could hit those notes with such clarity as he sang "Morgen, Morgen, One More Day Without You", which was originally a German song.' The song was a hit in Germany for Ivo Robic in 1959, and also made the US Top 20 that year. An English version of the song, with the translated title 'One More Sunrise', was a UK Top 20 hit for Dickie Valentine in late 1959. Vera Lynn also recorded a popular version of the song.

'Brendan was also singing other great ballads such as "Boolavogue" or the Gospel song "The Holy City" – all that stuff. Such a fantastic voice. Meanwhile, Tom Dunphy was doing all the country stuff. Jim Conlon on guitar was another great musician, as were Eddie Sullivan and Gerry Cullen. Charlie Matthews of course had hits of his own, and Michael Coppinger on sax was a great player. They were a brilliant all-round band,' says Paddy.

While admiring The Royal Showband as a star-struck teenager, Paddy didn't envisage that he would eventually play with Brendan and Tom in Las Vegas.

'I remember seeing them on another night in The Embassy Ballroom in Castleblayney, on a Wednesday night when we weren't working. I picked up the courage to go into the band room afterwards to talk to them. They were all very friendly fellows. I often look back on that night, when I wasn't even dreaming of ever working with some of them, in Las Vegas of all places!

'There were a lot of musicians in other bands who didn't make it as big as they should have. The showband scene had so many great musicians,' says Paddy. When the showband phenomenon was at its peak in Ireland, it was said that the country had over 700 bands. They crisscrossed the country, and also played at Irish emigrant venues in the UK and the USA.

As well as entertaining the Irish at home and abroad, the scene also employed approximately 6,000 people, between musicians, managers and road crews. But when Paddy started playing in The Maurice Lynch Band, in the mid-1950s, it was a much smaller scene.

Admission charges to the small halls were minuscule by today's prices. 'It was usually half a crown [two shillings and six pence]. It might be put up to three shillings in some places, and there would be uproar. Later, when the showbands came along, it was seven shillings and six pence for the big dances. But I remember a protest outside a hall in Cork when they put the admission price up to ten shillings. This was years after I left Castleblayney, when I was with The Capitol Showband. The protest was outside The Arcadia Ballroom where the price was usually seven shillings and six pence. The promoter had put it up to ten shillings on New Year's Eve, and people were walking up and down outside protesting.'

During the 1950s, The Maurice Lynch Band mostly played in small halls, but they played some bigger venues too. 'We would play some Wednesday nights in Barry's Hotel in Lower Denmark Street in Dublin, to maybe up to 400 people in the early days. Later, we played with Maurice's band in The Olympic Ballroom, also in Dublin, and there would be 1,200 to 1,400 dancers. That was at the "Ags" dance, run by a committee of mostly agricultural science students.

'We also played at a lot of carnivals around the country, including a few as far away from our home as Galway. One was in Milltown I think, and another in Dunmore, the home town of the Donnellan brothers, the famous Galway footballers of the 1960s. Those were long journeys, and the carnivals usually went on until two in the morning. So by the time we were heading home it was very late, especially for any musicians who were working the next day, as some in our band did, including my dad. But for those of us who were young at the time, we never seemed to care.'

As well as their love of music, Paddy and his father also shared a passion for fishing. No doubt living so close to Lough Muckno fuelled Paddy's interest in fishing from childhood.

'Most of the men that I knew growing up fished in the evening time, for perch or pike. It was a lovely, relaxed pastime. My father often fished for trout, and he used to tie his own flies. He was a fly fisherman and taught me how to fish with the fly in the rivers and lake around home.

'I will always remember one occasion when we were fishing for trout after a heavy shower of rain and there was a bit of a flow in the river. I was fishing with a worm as a bait that day when I hooked this big trout. I was playing it and trying to get it on to the riverbank when my father came and got the net under it, and we eventually landed it. It was over three pounds in weight, and for wild trout around our area that was considered a big fish.

'My father put the fish on the floor of the car and its colour looked magnificent with some moss from the riverbank around it. The whole way back to Castleblayney I was admiring the trout, delighted with myself for having hooked it. Then my father got out on the main street, with his waders still on him, and he was stopped for a chat by a local businessman.

The shopkeeper said to him, "Any luck with the fishing, Paddy?" and my father replied, "Yeah, the young fellow hooked a great trout." When the businessman came over and saw the trout, he did a deal there and then, giving us ten shillings for it. I was unhappy about selling the fish, but I was aware that ten shillings was a lot of money. There was nothing fishy about his offer, and the moment he mentioned ten shillings the trout was gone,' laughs Paddy.

During school holidays, Paddy would travel with his father to some of the small post offices. 'It was great for me to go with Dad in the mail van during the summer. There was a place in Latton where we might have to wait two or three hours for the mail to be ready. We would spend the time fishing for trout, but if it was a wet day, we practised the saxophone.'

Can you picture, in your mind's eye, the strange scene of two men sitting in a mail van on a side road in Leitrim on a wet afternoon, blowing for all they were worth into saxophones? It shows the love they had for the music that if, by chance, they were left waiting for the mail, they would have the instruments with them, ready to play.

When travelling with the band, conversation between his father and himself would either be about music or fishing. Tall tales were often told among band members about 'the biggest fish in the world', the one that 'always' broke the fishing rod and got away!

Musically, Paddy Junior became the big fish that left the local band in 1960, but before that his father had retired from his day job and from the band. 'He had retired from the band a few months before I left. He was more or less retired from the day job at that time as well. Dad was delighted to have more time to do his trout fishing and stuff like that. Thank God he had time at that stage to enjoy his pastimes a little bit more.'

Leaving The Maurice Lynch Band created some ill feeling, but Paddy got an offer that he simply could not refuse. 'When I got the offer from The Capitol Showband, I knew that this was going fully professional into music. I knew music was going to be my life, and I grabbed at that. I was happy in The Maurice Lynch Band, but I felt I had to take the offer.

'I think Maurice was a bit disappointed when I left. But many years later, when I had a pub in Castleblayney, Maurice would come down and play at the Monday night music sessions there. I was so thrilled about that, because he was the last person in the world that I would have any ill feeling for. He started me off in the business while I was still at school, and he was a great guy.'

'Maurice taught me my trade as a young fellow, and the girls used to be mad about me back then,' said Paddy in an interview with Marty Whelan on the RTÉ TV programme 'Open House' in 2002.

So, there may be a sliver of truth in a tale recounted in Tim Ryan's 1995 book *Tell Roy Rogers I'm Not In*. It states that when demolishing the old Embassy Ballroom, the builders found some slogans daubed on one of the walls. One piece of graffiti read, 'Paddy Cole courted a woman up against this wall.'

'I won't elaborate on any of those things,' says Paddy now. 'I still want to get an odd plate of spuds at home now and again, instead of a plate over my head.'

Chapter 4

The Capitol Come Calling for Cole in the Capital

The showband craze reached its zenith in Ireland in the early 1960s, with Brendan Bowyer and The Royal Showband streaking ahead of the rest. But they were soon to be challenged by a hand-picked band of musicians called The Capitol.

'Ireland up to then could be a dreary enough place, with not a lot of entertainment apart from the parish hall dance and an odd night at the movies. But then came the showbands, and my God, you could dance six or seven nights a week,' said Paddy in RTÉ's *A Little Bit Showband* in 2011.

The showbands were an integral part of the soundtrack to the social, cultural and economic fabric of a rapidly changing, more progressive and vibrant Ireland. An energised and very different country emerged, and with it a highly professional music scene.

In tandem with the changing, swinging sixties, the career of Paddy Cole changed too. He was headhunted for one of Ireland's biggest and most success-ful showbands on two occasions before he finally agreed to move to Dublin.

The Capitol first came knocking on Paddy's door at an 'Ags' dance in the capital. 'As two of the original line-up did not want to go full-time into music, they were seeking replacements. I was one of those that had caught their attention. It seems that they had been watching my performance with The Maurice Lynch Band for some time. Hand-picking musicians like this was a completely new way of starting a band in Ireland at that time.'

In 2011, on *A Little Bit Showband*, Paddy said that this customising of musicians for different band roles was a big change. 'Before that, a band from Athlone had all members from around Athlone, a band from Derry had all members from Derry and so on. I was lucky enough to be picked as the sax and clarinet player in the band'.

The two men behind this new showband were university students in Dublin. They were on a committee that organised the Ags (for Agricultural Science students) 'hops' or dances, held regularly in the Olympic Ballroom.

Eamon Monahan hailed from a musical family in Donegal, and played piano in what was originally known as The Capitol Quartet. In Galway, Des and his brother Johnny Kelly played in a family band called The Quicksil-ver. Their sister Bernie was also in the group. When Des moved to Dublin and met Eamon Monahan, they decided to put musicians from different parts of Ireland together in a band.

While Paddy's father encouraged him to take up the offer, his mother wasn't pleased with the idea of her only son going off to live in a flat in big bad Dublin all on his own, with nobody to look after him!

'When I got the first offer, I said I was going,' says Paddy. 'But then my mother started to have reservations about me leaving Castleblayney to live alone in Dublin. I have often described it as a bit like a "Rip Kirby" case – you had to watch out the next day for the next instalment.' Rip Kirby was a popular detective comic strip, published in many newspapers from the 1940s onwards. The reader was left hanging after each episode, waiting for the following edition of the newspaper or magazine to discover what would happen. Those in the know in the music business of 1960, were waiting on tenterhooks too regarding rumours of Paddy Cole joining The Capitol. Would he or wouldn't he?

'I was going, then I wasn't going, and word went out in the music business that I had turned down the job. Other fellows were getting on to the two boys in The Capitol to see if the job was still vacant. Then Eamon Monahan and Des Kelly arrived down at my parents' house one day to talk with my mother about it. They sat down with her and reassured her. The local doctor, Dr Healy, and the local pharmacist, Mrs Leavy, who were friends of my mother's, also spoke to her about the great opportunity that it was. They told her that this could be the biggest showband in the business and that it was a career move not to be missed.'

The wages of £30 per week were something that very few young fellows would turn down back in 1961. It was a fortune in an Ireland where thousands were emigrating to jobs in the UK and America, usually for more back-breaking work than playing music.

'The wages I was offered starting off were four or five times what my father was earning for a week's work in the post office. So, it was a case of when ya gotta go, ya gotta go,' he says.

It was a big career move, but Paddy says that he was undaunted. 'I was very enthusiastic about it, because I had heard the band playing in Swan Park Ballroom in Monaghan, and I thought they were great. The guys on saxophone and trombone had decided they were not going professional, and so two vacancies had arisen. Don Long and I were picked as the two replacements.'

Don was a jazz player, and a third member of the band, Paul Sweeney, was also into jazz, so Paddy says it was easy for him to gel with the band. 'As three of us were into the same sort of music, it made it easier to fit in. Don was a recognised player in Cork, where he had played with all the top jazz bands. I had never heard him play before, and had never met him, but when we were together at the first rehearsals, I was extremely impressed.

'At that time, there were no relief bands or support acts, so we would play for at least five hours per night. But the first hour of The Capitol Showband's programme was mostly Dixieland jazz, and fans who liked jazz music would come along earlier to hear that Dixieland session. Paul, Don and I were on the same wavelength from the start.'

Rehearsals were demanding, because they were not going to use music stands – each member had to memorise all of the parts he was playing. 'You might be playing a harmony line, which wasn't so easy to memorise. We just got used to it – it was part of our job and we had to knuckle down to it. A lot of the time, we rehearsed in the ballrooms we would be playing in that night. We arrived early and spent a few hours rehearsing. Then we'd take a break for something to eat before coming back to do the gig. It was all time-consuming. If we had been using music stands, it would have been a lot easier just to write out our parts and read them. However, it was the new style and we were part of that new style.

'It was glamorous, and we were enjoying it all, even if we weren't that conscious of how good the music was. We thought it would go on forever. In the Capitol Showband, we were well looked after. We had a customised touring bus with reclining aeroplane seats, which a big luxury back then. It was custom-built for us by George Duffy in Dundalk, who was a musician himself with his own band. He went on to make band wagons for other showbands.

'We also stayed over in hotels, which eliminated a lot of the long journeys. There was a road manager with us, Sean Jordan, and Jim Doherty – who was managing the band out of the office in Dublin – travelled to many of the dates as well. So, it was very well organised from a management and logistics point of view. All we had to do was arrive, do our rehearsals and play the music.'

Paddy's first gig with The Capitol was near his home, at the Pavilion Ballroom in Blackrock, County Louth, but he came close to missing it. 'As you can imagine, a lot of people from my home area would be there. We rehearsed that week, but on the day before the gig, I developed a streptococcal throat. Luckily the boys in the band knew a doctor who had been a student with them in Dublin, and he gave me a few injections that evening. It was a worry for me – if I didn't show up at the dance in Blackrock, so near to my home, the locals would say that I was spoofing about being in the band,' he laughs.

'Anyway, the injections did the trick and I was okay to play the dance. It was packed to capacity. In fact, there were as many people outside as there were inside, so we got off to a fantastic start.'

Any lingering doubts that Paddy might have had about making the right career move were largely dispelled that night. 'While I loved working in The Maurice Lynch Band, I felt I had to make the career move to Dublin at that time. I suppose I always had a longing to go back home to Castleblayney, and on any nights we had off I tended to go home. I always visited Castleblayney regularly, as I do to this day, going back to visit with my sisters and their families. But I never really considered going back to what I had been doing, and there never was a plan B. Maybe there should have been a plan B!

'But it was so hectic in those early days with The Capitol that there wasn't even time to think. We were here, there and everywhere, doing photo shoots, newspaper interviews, radio interviews … We were constantly playing, and we had our own radio programme on Radio Luxembourg. We would record that in the Tommy Ellis Studio in Dublin. All those things kept us going non-stop. I was sharing a house with the drummer, Johnny Kelly, and we got into a routine there as well.'

Paddy's mother's insistence on ensuring that her only son was okay in Dublin sometimes resulted in him being slagged off as the typical country boy in the city. 'While it might have embarrassed me a bit at times, I usually took little notice of it. In the goodness of her heart, my mother would send up stuff to me with anyone travelling anywhere near to where we were staying in Dublin. Or if we were playing near home, she would arrive with half a dozen duck eggs and some brown bread. I used to get a terrible slating from the other boys about this – especially about the duck eggs! She reckoned that the duck eggs were better for me than hen eggs, but sure half the time I couldn't tell her that they weren't used at all.'

While they lived in Dublin, and The Capitol quickly attracted capacity crowds to venues in the capital, Cork was a much harder city for them to make an impact in. But The Capitol finally did crack Cork, attracting over 4,000 fans to the Arcadia Ballroom, which Paddy says was an amazing venue to play in.

'The stage was up as high as a balcony would be in other halls. The gig was challenging, because The Dixies from Cork were the popular resident band there. They were local, the dancers loved them, and musician Steve Lynch did some amazing feats while playing – things like hanging over the balcony by his legs while playing "Guitar Boogie Shuffle" at the same time.

'So, competition was hot, as The Dixies were a great band even before they went on the road full-time. A lot of bands spoke about how everyone was up against it trying to compete with The Dixies in Cork. You had to be on your toes, because they played so well and put on such a show that every other band had to put on a big performance to equal them.'

But when The Capitol finally cracked Cork, they remained popular in the southern capital for the rest of the band's career. 'Cork was a huge place for us after that. We always had big crowds there.' And Paddy went on to become a huge success himself at the Cork Jazz Festival years later.

The Capitol scored another notable success, shortly after being established, by being one of the first showbands to have a fan club. Paddy says that at the time he hardly knew what a fan club was!

'It was operated by two girls – Maura Hurley, Lord have mercy on her, as she has passed away, and Monica McNelis, who now lives in Belgium. Strange to say, when doing my radio show on Sunshine Radio in Dublin recently, we got an email from Monica. I was just after playing a song by Butch Moore and The Capitol when an email arrived in the station.

She said she was listening in Belgium, and hearing Butch and The Capitol on the show brought back happy memories for her.

'Monica and Maura did unbelievable work to make the band popular in the early days. At that time, I don't know if any other showband had a fan club, but those girls established it. They sent out brochures and letters to the fans, and updates about what we were doing. One time, they organised a train full of fans to go from Dublin to Carlow for one of our gigs. It was a special train you could hire, and I think some other bands also did so. One of those was the Johnny Flynn Band, who also had a special train taking fans from Dublin to Dundalk.

'This was a time of very few phones in homes. There were no mobile phones or fax machines, no computers and no Google,' says Paddy with a smile. 'The two girls in our fan club were fantastic. They wrote letters to fans and sent out all the promotional stuff, postcard photos of the band, and so on. It was almost a full-time job, but they were doing it in their spare time, while also working at their own jobs in Dublin. When they first asked if they could start a fan club, I don't think any of us knew what a fan club was. They were way ahead of their time.'

In 1960, as The Capitol were formed in Dublin, across the Irish Sea in Liverpool, a few lads named The Beatles were about to explode onto the worldwide music scene. The meteoric rise of the fab four from Liverpool resulted in a huge shift in music tastes. It was a hindrance rather than a help for record sales of big bands such as The Capitol.

'Of course, we were very aware of how brilliant those boys were. But unfortunately we didn't pick up on the changes it would mean for music tastes. We were doing a lot of the Bill Haley rock'n'roll stuff, which used a lot of brass. Suddenly, there were only four guys with guitars in the most popular group in the world. Maybe we were a little snobbish at that stage, not realising how great The Beatles were. We realised what fantastic musicians they were and the brilliant stuff they wrote. But it was only when we tried to break into Britain with our records, we saw that music tastes had changed.

'That was later, after we had played the London Palladium and promoter Phil Solomon tried to break us into the British record scene. Some Irish girls working in a record shop in London's Camden Town told one of our lads that the powers-that-be had told them to stop stocking records except those by four-piece groups. That was the coming trend, started by The Beatles.

'That record stores directive came at a bad time for us. We were ready to start flooding the English market with recordings, which we had spent a lot of money on. Those records were well produced, but none of the UK shops wanted to stock them. The new trend was towards groups such as The Beatles, The Rolling Stones, The Animals and other similar acts. The Mersey Beat changed the music business for everyone, and perhaps we didn't pick up on it as quickly as we should have.'

At home in Ireland, however, The Capitol were still packing the dance-halls. Paddy says that all the band members had a say in compiling their live show. 'We all made suggestions regarding what we should be playing in our live programme. It was a mixed bag, and we were also guided by what was in the charts at the time. At times our suggestions were accepted and at other times not, but we all meant well and there was a team spirit in the band. Everybody was respected for their input, but invariably a final decision was made by band leader Des Kelly. Sometimes we might spend a day or two rehearsing tunes that we thought were fabulous. But if they didn't make the charts or become popular, we would drop them. So that was time wasted.'

On their first tour of the UK, The Capitol played all the top ballrooms. They quickly established themselves, particularly in the Irish dancehalls around London. 'The band also became hugely popular very quickly in the other cities with big Irish populations, including Manchester and Birmingham. But so great was our popularity in the London area that we could play in halls there for a few weeks at a time. Many of the fans followed us around from venue to venue, as they would do at home, and all the dances were packed out. A man named Frank McLoone did the booking for the promoters. He was a genius at placing the right bands in the halls where they drew the biggest crowds. He would know an area where a country band would do better than a pop band. Frank McLoone, God rest him, was a great friend of mine and he could identify what bands were best for touring in England.

'It was easier on those of us who were single than those who were married to go off on tours to America or England. Only on reflection now can I see how hard it was for a musician with a wife and children to head off on such tours.'

The popularity of The Capitol Showband soared in Dublin City from early on, and Paddy remembers big queues of fans waiting for the doors to open. 'Not meaning to sound big-headed, but it was great to see crowds lining the streets when we arrived to play at the Crystal or the Olympic ballrooms in Dublin. Sometimes a queue might be up to 500 yards long and maybe four deep, waiting to get in. Other times it was embarrassing, because somebody you knew from home would shout at you from the queue. But we couldn't do anything about bringing them in. We might have spirited an odd one in under our coats from time to time,' he laughs.

'But it wasn't only The Capitol that had queues outside ballrooms. A lot of other showbands were also getting similar big crowds. They were exciting times, but unfortunately perhaps we took it a little bit for granted. I'd have to say that against ourselves. We may have thought the good times would last forever. But of course, everybody finds out that this is not the case.'

Paddy and the other showband musicians lived for the business seven nights a week. On their nights off, they would often go to watch other bands play.

In his 2010 book *Our Joe*, Eddie Rowley says that in the early 1960s Paddy Cole, then with the Capitol Showband, 'turned up out of curiosity to see the new singing sensation, Joe Dolan'. This was in the Ierne Ballroom on Dublin's Parnell Square. 'I loved him straight away. I loved his voice and what a worker he was on stage. I saw that from the word go.'

Paddy has many great memories of times spent in the company of the late Joe. Sometimes they met on TV or at radio shows, or in entertainment venues where either one was playing. They also socialised together, and as both men were golf fanatics, they often spent time on golf courses too.

Our Joe tells of a night when Joe and members of his band came to see The Capitol in Longford. Paddy and a few others from The Capitol went back to Joe's house 'till eight or nine in the morning. Paddy says that Joe was a 'rascal' in many ways, but such a loveable person. He recalls a time in 2002 when they were both guests of Marty Whelan and Mary Kennedy on 'Open House' RTÉ 1. On the show, Joe firstly praised Paddy and then put a twist in the tail of his words of praise.

'Paddy Cole is probably the most unbelievable person you could ever meet. I have never heard Paddy say anything rude about anybody or talk behind anyone's back, or really cut up anybody. He is just one of those lovely people that come around once in your lifetime. We even play a round of golf now and again. But my first memory of Paddy was when The Capitol Showband came to play in the County Hall in Mullingar. I did not really want to go at all, but my mother dragged me along,' said Joe to loud laughter and applause. Paddy quickly replied, 'He builds you up and then he gives you the knife,' to more laughter and applause.

Paddy still laughs about this wisecrack by Joe. 'He would often say to me that his mother took him to see The Capitol for the first time when he was only in short pants. He was such a great guy. We did a few TV shows together. He was a guest on my *Craic'n'Cole* show for RTÉ, and you would always be guaranteed a great bit of craic doing any show with Joe.

'We became great friends, and even when Helen and I lived in Castleblayney, we would drive to Dublin for a night out with Joe. When we played golf together, there was always a bet of a tenner, which was never paid. We tried at one time to figure out who owed the most to the other.

'On a sadder note, a few weeks before he died, Joe phoned me after getting out of hospital. He was positive about things. I said that as I was a member of Lahinch Golf Club, they would love to see him playing down there. Joe, being the modest man that he was, said, "Do ya think so, Paddy?" I told him that with the help of God, when the weather would pick up, I would bring him to Lahinch. I assured him that he would be treated like royalty there. He replied that he was looking forward to going there for the golf, but sadly, three weeks later he was dead.'

Paddy says he will never forget the winter's day when Joe was taken to his final resting place through the streets of Mullingar. 'I stood on the side of a street as thousands of people sang "Goodbye Venice, Goodbye", and it would have drawn a tear from a stone. I unashamedly cried too.'

Joe Dolan, Paddy and Paul Sweeney, playing with the local band in Florida, on a Sean Skehan-organised golf trip.

The showband scene was a great grounding for both artists. Both Joe Dolan and Paddy Cole played in Las Vegas, but at different times. Paddy eventually went to live and entertain in Vegas for almost five years. Joe Dolan went in the opposite direction, topping pop charts all over Europe. His 'Make Me an Island' reached number three in the UK and number two in South Africa. It was a top 10 pop hit in four other European countries, including number two in Belgium, and was a hit in over a dozen countries.

As well as having massive hits in the UK and around Europe, Joe also became a big star in the then USSR, playing to thousands of fans in places such as Moscow and St Petersburg. In 1978, Joe was the first Irish star, and perhaps only the second from the western world, to tour in communist Russia, before the end of the Cold War period. (The *New York Times* credits US country star the late George Hamilton IV as the first American singer to tour Russia, a few years earlier. He played in Moscow on 28 March 1974.)

'Joe's international success was a credit to the showband era, like that of many other singers and musicians from that scene,' says Paddy.

Showbands have come in for criticism in more recent times, including from Boomtown Rat Bob Geldof. 'Showbands were crap,' said Geldof. 'Musically, they were a death.' (*From Paddydom to Punk, From a Whisper to a Scream*, RTÉ 1, March 2000) But Paddy says that this is a little unfair. 'Some people thought it was the hip thing to do a few years back to knock the showbands. But a lot of the guys that were in showbands moved on to play in the RTÉ orchestras, or in the resident bands on the *Late Late Show* or the *Pat Kenny Show*. Stephen Travers of the Miami put manners on Geldof when he sent a message to him challenging him to a competition playing bass. Stephen said he would play bass against him and that seemed to have shut him up, as he did not react to the challenge.'

(Stephen Travers was a survivor of the Miami Showband massacre, when three of his band colleagues were murdered while returning from a gig in Banbridge, County Down. In one of the many gruesome atrocities of the 'Troubles' in Northern Ireland, the musicians were gunned down by loyalist paramilitaries on 31 July 1975. Stephen was seriously wounded, but survived the hail of bullets by pretending to be dead in a ditch. He is acknowledged as one of many brilliant musicians from the showband scene.)

'Guys such as Geldof, who were knocking the showbands, probably never heard a showband,' says Paddy. 'I doubt he ever saw one play live. It might seem to be the cool thing to do to knock the showbands and assume they all had bad musicians. But a lot of great musicians, such as Stephen Travers, Rory Gallagher and many more, came through the showband scene.'

Chapter 5

Drink, But No Drugs, and Rock'n'Roll

Like a rocket launched from the then Cape Canaveral (Cape Kennedy after 1963), the Capitol Showband took off into the showband stratosphere of the 1960s. With a line-up of Des and Johnny Kelly, Eamon Monahan, Butch Moore, Paddy Cole, Don Long, Jimmy Hogan, Paul Sweeney and later Bram McCarthy, they had double the numbers of The Beatles to woo the fans.

With President John F Kennedy in situ in The White House, the first Catholic US President of Irish descent, Irish emigrants were flying high in the States, and so were The Capitol. Only a year after their establishment, the band were given a civic reception by the Mayor of New York, another man of Irish descent, at the start of their first US tour.

The ballrooms they played in during that first and subsequent US tours were packed, just like the dance halls were at home. Back home, as the good times rolled on for the band members, they drove fashionable cars, wore smart suits, started drinking and doing devilment on each other and no doubt attracted the girls!

But Paddy says that the scourge of drugs, which later ruined many a good musician's life, were not a part of the Irish music scene at that time. 'The only ones needing drugs were fans who might have to take an odd Aspro or Anadin tablet to ease a headache if we were playing too loud,' he laughs.

The American tours were not 'nine-to-five' jobs. It was more like 9am to 2am every day of almost non-stop work. They did endless radio and newspaper interviews and photo shoots in between travel, soundchecks and gigs. That first US tour saw them playing in New York, Chicago, Boston and San Francisco. Then they doubled back to play second dates in Chicago, Boston and New York before flying home.

At least they had the comfort of aeroplane travel in the US. At home, the schedule was more punishing. Though in their comfortable, custom-built bus, they still travelled far and wide, often along rugged country roads. They would start out before midday, almost every day, and after rehearsals in an empty hall, they would play 'from 9pm to 1 or 2am, without a full break', says Paddy. 'Half the band would go off for a short break and a cup of tea and a sandwich while the other half played on. On the return of the first four, the others would do the same. There was little or no drinking, except occasionally when a ballroom proprietor might leave a few bottles of stout in the dressing room.' Paddy was a non-drinker for his first three years in the band.

While he says he took his first alcoholic drinks in 1964, it was still only a few bottles of Guinness. The heavy drinking culture, often wrongly associated with music groups, was not prevalent among The Capitol Showband's members in those days.

They band received a welcome befitting major music stars in New York. 'The Lord Mayor of Dublin at the time, Ben Briscoe, was a cousin of the Mayor of New York. He had sent word to him and we got an unbelievable reception. We were guests at New York City Hall and the Mayor there really rolled out the red carpet for us.

'When we arrived at the first gig, in the City Centre Ballroom, owned by Irish promoter Bill Fuller, the crowds were waiting outside for us. We arrived in taxis from the hotel, not far away from the ballroom, and it was like a scene from back home outside the New York ballroom, with these throngs of people waiting to go in. It was a wonderful feeling. The hall held about 4,000 people, and there was a resident band as well. That was a requirement of the American musician's union – that there would be an American band as a support act.'

After the phenomenal success of their first US date, the band travelled by plane to Chicago, Boston and San Francisco. 'It was a long haul across to California, but stopping off and playing in Chicago, both on the outgoing and return journeys, made it easier. We did a full weekend in Chicago again on the way back, before going on to Boston, which was only a hop away from New York for the second set of gigs. All the dances were packed, including Chicago, which seemed so far away for us to draw a crowd.

But Gene O'Hagan, who worked with Bill Fuller's organisation, had all the pre-tour publicity done in the Irish-American newspapers and the radio stations there.'

The Capitol's first US tour in 1961 was during the six weeks of Lent, when dancing was not allowed in Ireland under the strict Catholic rules of that time. 'Dancing was allowed in Northern Ireland, but not in the South during Lent. Of course, all the small ballrooms and parish halls on the Northern side of the border were cleaning up with the big crowds during Lent. There is one story from that time about the plight of one professional musician in Cork who protested about not being allowed to work during the six weeks of Lent. He would arrive up to the Bishop's palace with his six children at the start of Lent and ask the Bishop every year how he was going to get money to feed his kids for the next six weeks. He would cause a bit of a stir at the start of Lent every year. But he was a lone voice in the wilderness, as he was the only guy who was giving out about the ban. But he had the courage of his convictions.'

Bigger bands, such as The Capitol, were lucky that they could choose to play big venues in the UK or the US during Lent, but others were not so fortunate. 'Other bands had to go abroad and play in small venues or pubs just to survive during Lent.'

The Capitol made many trips to the USA after their initial foray, and the big crowds were always there to greet them. 'We went a few times a year, and then we started going to Toronto in Canada as well. That was an unusual one, as we played in the same venue there every time. It was a most beautiful spot called The Maple Leaf Ballroom. The crowds were always big, and most of the crowd came from Northern Ireland. I heard it said that at one time, Toronto had more Orange halls than there were in Belfast.

But all the dancers mixed, and we never saw any animosity, as music was a unifying force among all the Irish there.'

Back home, and just a year into the life of The Capitol Showband, the first change of personnel came when Paul Sweeney quit to go back to college. Paul had studied art in college, and then decided to go back and study architecture. Don Long from Cork suggested that Bram McCarthy, also from Cork, would be an ideal replacement on trumpet. Bram was a brilliant trumpet player, and a great reader of music, who played with resident bands in Cork hotels. 'It was a great decision,' says Paddy. 'Bram was a brilliant all-round musician and a lovely singer. He could also play the Dixieland jazz, and when we were rehearsing, he was very quick to pick up every tune. He came in and took over from Paul, and it was all seamless –as if there was no change.'

The new ballrooms that suddenly dotted the Irish landscape in the 1960s were big barns of venues, with little or no heating. Heating wasn't needed, as the crowds were so big that you would 'roast' in them at night. But they could be cold, dreary places for rehearsals during wintertime, according to Paddy.

'We would set up the equipment and try it out for sound quality. Then we would play, on a record player, listening attentively, any new song we were due to practise, and learn off our parts. It was slow, tedious work, and as I said earlier, if we had been writing out the music and reading it, the practice sessions would have been much faster. It wasn't always cold for rehearsals – in the summertime, it might be so warm that we would have to open the side doors. We might even scare all the sheep and cattle in neighbouring fields with our rehearsals.'

After going to the local hotel for their evening meal and to 'freshen up', the band members would come back to a packed ballroom, full of fans, smoke, sweat and dust. 'Ballrooms were roasting in summer, and warm in winter too if the band was attracting big enough crowds. There is a famous story told in show business circles about a singer who said to a ballroom owner that it was very cold in his hall. The proprietor replied, "If ye were drawing big enough of a crowd, it wouldn't be cold," and that ended that talk.'

On the RTÉ programme *A Little Bit Showband*, Paddy said that in some ballrooms you could see nothing from the stage but 'a mass of people plus smoke and dust rising from the floor'. Such scenes are still clearly etched in his mind. 'Everybody was smoking, including the band. Standing on the stage in some of those ballrooms, we couldn't see the back wall of the ballroom due to the cloud of smoke. Almost everybody there, ladies and gents, were smoking. What a wonderful change it is nowadays that one can go into gatherings in a theatre, restaurant, hall, pub or hotel and everything is crystal clear for all to see since the smoking ban. It must have been very unhealthy for everyone during our days playing in the dancehalls.

'I remember scenes during the summer when the ballroom staff would go around with a long staff to open the high windows of the halls. Sometimes all the side doors might have to be opened as well. You would see the smoke, dust and steam being blown out into the clear summer night air. It must have looked like the place was on fire for people watching from a distance.'

Paddy says that the showband years and the ballrooms were a big contributor to the economy of Ireland. 'The days of the dances were of particular benefit to local business. Hairdressers would have the ladies coming in to get their hair styled. Drapery shops – later it was boutiques – would have the ladies also visiting to buy new outfits. The shops supplying the ballrooms with soft drinks and sandwiches also benefited, plus all the staff that worked in the ballrooms. There was also a boost for local filling stations, as many of the hundreds of cars coming into a town or village would fill up with petrol for the return journeys. Taxis and hackney services also benefited, taking fans to and from dances, as did coach-hire companies. Everyone was benefiting. It was an awful shame that an industry such as the showband scene ended up being let slip away.'

As the rural ballrooms did not have bars, 'there was truly little drinking, and people didn't have the price of it anyway.' Paddy only took his first drink in 1964. That was at the launch of the band's first record, titled 'Foolin' Time'. It was written by Phil Coulter from Derry, who was to achieve great things on the international music scene in the following years.

'Late one night in Bundoran in the summer of 1963, I had a phone call that changed my life,' wrote Phil Coulter in a booklet published by K-Tel Records in 1984 ('Butch Moore and The Capitol Showband – A Souvenir Programme'). A friend of Phil's told him that members of The Capitol Showband would be at his gig in a hotel that night.

Paddy Cole vividly remembers how the band first got to know the young Derry songwriter. 'We became great friends with a young Phil Coulter and a young Paul Brady when we met them in Bundoran. We would do a weekend at a time of dances there during the summer season. Phil was playing in a hotel in Bundoran, and even when our dance had finished in the early hours, we would go down to the hotel and a music session would start up. That's how we first met Phil and Paul Brady. Phil would be playing the piano, and Paul would join in on the session with his guitar and banjo. Phil was a student in Queen's University, Belfast, at that time. He was writing songs, and he knew someone who got a demo copy of his song 'Foolin' Time' pressed. He gave it to us, and after listening to it, Butch recorded it and it became our first hit.'

The song went to number three in the Irish Top 20 in February 1964 for Butch Moore and The Capitol. To this day, Phil Coulter says that was the song that started off his career as an international songwriter and performer, and without The Capitol it would never have happened.

'Phil also produced the record for us, and it was the first piece of music that Phil Coulter ever had recorded. He went on to do great things, including co-writing the Eurovision hit "Puppet on a String" for Sandi Shaw in 1967.'

Success didn't follow-up immediately for Phil Coulter and The Capitol, however. The next song he wrote for the band was a flop. It was called 'I Missed You', and it missed the charts completely, even though Phil said he loved the baritone sax solo by Paddy on it. 'I think we were trying to be a little bit too clever with the arrangement on that song. It was a very tricky arrangement and there were a lot of stops in it, when people just wanted a song to dance to,' says Paddy.

But the links between Phil Coulter and The Capitol continued, and it was to benefit both sides in their progress internationally. 'We are still very friendly today,' says Paddy. 'He phones me regularly. Back then, we were doing our UK trips for a big agent in London named Phil Solomon. He also had an agency for people who were writing songs, and as he was looking for a new songwriter, we suggested Phil Coulter. Des Kelly told Phil, and he got in touch with the agency in England, and that is how it all started for him there. He was a very able guy and an ambitious person. But he has said many times that only for the break with Phil Solomon's office in England, he probably would have ended up teaching music in Queen's University. It's amazing how one event like that can swing a person's life in a different direction.'

Paddy aged twelve, 'Ireland's youngest saxophone player',
playing an American plastic saxophone.

Above: Paddy, early 1940s, Castleblayney.
Left: Paddy, age seven, with three of his sisters, Mai, Sadie and Carmel, at home in Castleblayney.

Above: A promotional photo of The Capitol Showband.
Below: A more relaxed-looking Capitol Showband: back: Jimmy Hogan, Don Long, Eamon Monahan, Paddy, Butch Moore; front: Johnny Kelly, Paul Sweeney, Des Kelly.

Left: Helen and the kids relaxing on a sunny day in Las Vegas.
Below: Pat Cole with his friend 'Junior' and Karen, Las Vegas, 1973.

Above: The Big 8 on stage. Paddy would play all the instruments on the rack in front, and finally whip the tin whistle out of his pocket.
Below: Butch Moore, famous American bandleader Woody Herman and Paddy.

Above: With Twink on an RTÉ television show, 1980s.
Below: With the parade Grand Marshall at the 1985 St Patrick's Day parade, New York.

Right: Paddy on baritone sax. Below: Maurice Lynch, Paddy's sister Lucia Chisholm and presenter Donncha Ó Dúlaing in Castleblayney in 1980, during the making of RTÉ's documentary *Donncha's Travelling Roadshow*, about the town's well-known musicians.

Paul Brady also went on to international success as a singer/songwriter. Shortly after those late-night music sessions with The Capitol in Bundoran, he joined the folk group The Johnstons. They had a number one in 1966 with 'The Travelling People', and another Top 20 hit the following year with 'The Curragh of Kildare'.

As the money rolled in during his early days in The Capitol, Paddy and other band members started buying fancy cars. 'Some of the lads bought bigger models than me, but I had a liking for VW Beatles. The first one I bought was a second-hand one, costing £315. It was ZX4834, and I couldn't tell you the number of my own car parked outside the door now,' he laughs.

He says that 'being a cute Monaghan man', he would have bargained with the car salesman to get it for £300. 'But before I could do so, Eamon Monahan, who was with me, said, "that's a good price – we will take it." I nearly fainted. As they say in my home area, I would have been "dealing" with him, to get the price down.'

Another shock was in store for Paddy when he drove home to Castleblayney and parked outside his parents' front door. 'My mother asked me, who owns the VW Beatle parked outside? When I told her it was mine, she questioned me regarding where I got the money. I said that it was easy to get a loan from a bank in Dublin. It was late evening time, and I remember that she called all the family together to go on our knees and say the Rosary.' It was being offered that evening to God, seeking divine intervention to help Paddy pay off the money he had borrowed to buy the car! 'She was so shocked that I would be borrowing money from a bank. My mother was of the old school. She was a firm believer in pay as you go, and if you can't pay for it, then don't go.'

Paddy later bought a second VW Beetle – this time a new one – and he also bought a car for his father. 'To be honest, my dad's car was a second-hand one. I didn't go overboard with the spending, taking cognisance of the reception I got in Castleblayney when I arrived with the first car! When I traded in the first VW, I bought a new white one, SZD12. I got the flashy rim embellishers and all sorts of extras on that one.

'But some of the lads in the band went for bigger cars. They were driving Mercedes and Jaguars, and Eamon Monahan even had a Citroen. One of the features of that model was that it would sit down on its suspension at night. You pressed a button in the morning and it came back up. But it got to a stage with Eamon that while it would still sit down and go back up at the press of a button, it wouldn't go forwards or backwards. So, he had to get rid of it. I was happy with the VW Beetles. The two of them that I had were great cars.'

But Paddy wasn't wasting all his money on fancy cars. Like the Irish emigrants in England at the time, he was sending money home to his family every week. 'I came from a big family of six sisters and myself. My sister Sadie, Lord have mercy on her, was the eldest, and all the rest of them were younger than me. The youngest ones were all still at school when I moved to Dublin. I hardly knew my youngest sister Betty at all, as she was only a child when I left Castleblayney. I look back now on a photo from my wedding, and there is this little girl with a wee bonnet on her standing shyly at the side. That was my youngest sister Betty.

'The money I sent home every week helped the family. But some of my sisters, who are nearest to me in age, used to say that they were born at the wrong time. That was because, with me being able to help the family financially, they were able to send the younger girls to college, and they went on

Paddy Cole junior and senior with junior's first Mercedes.

to do great things. One of my sisters went to college in Cambridge, which was a big achievement back then. But they all did well, and we all keep in touch. We are a very united family, and we always were.'

The members of The Capitol were also a very united group in those early years, even if they did play pranks on each other. Paddy was probably the biggest prankster, and one of his biggest tricks was convincing lead singer Butch Moore that the tiny New York recording studio they were making their first record in was also where Elvis once recorded.

'Promoter Bill Fuller wanted me to record "Lagan Love" on the clarinet. He booked studio time in this studio in Manhattan, near the hotel where we were staying. Butch was also going to sing a few songs. I was first in, and I wrote, in the little cubicle where the singer recorded, the words, "Elvis Presley – hope I make it". Butch was such a lovely guy, but naïve though. When he saw this, he said to us, this must be one of New York's top studios. The rest of the band knew of my prank, and we all said, "Why is that so, Butch?" He replied, "Even Elvis must have been here in his early days, because he wrote something on the wall of the booth inside." But then Eamon Monahan shouted, "It was Paddy wrote that!" and there was murder! The session didn't finish, and the band nearly split over it,' laughs Paddy.

Paddy must have smiled years later at the thought of the Elvis incident, while chatting with 'The King' in his dressing room in Las Vegas! Indeed, the recording saga didn't end in New York, as Paddy explains:

'To make matters worse, my recording of "Lagan Love", which was recorded and later pressed into a single in New York, for the Irish market, was never released. Bill Fuller had thousands of copies of the single dispatched to Dublin Airport, but when import duty was levied on them,

Recording 'My Lagan Love' in New York.

he wouldn't pay it. They were probably left in some store in Dublin Airport till they were thrown out. However, a fan of The Capitol was working there, and he slipped out one box. So at least we got to hear the record. But I often thought that as Bill had gone to such expense in making the records, and then shipping them over, why not pay the duty in Dublin?'

Back in Dublin in the early 1960s, all pranks among band members were quickly forgotten as they worked together at becoming radio stars, with their own weekly programme on Radio Luxembourg. 'That show was done in conjunction with Phil Solomon. Des Kelly, plus others in management, felt this could help us break into the scene in the UK and possibly Europe. A lot of young people in Ireland listened to Radio Luxembourg at the time also. We had a fifteen-minute programme that went out once a week. But we had to pre-record the programme, in the Tommy Ellis Studio in Dublin, every Monday morning at 10am, no matter where we were the night before. It was a tough gig for us if we were playing over in the west of Ireland, up in Donegal or down in Kerry, on the Sunday night.

'The tunes and songs would be picked in advance, and we would also write out the parts beforehand. After the programme was recorded, the big reel of tape had to be physically delivered to the radio station. It wasn't like now, where you can press a button on a computer and it arrives instantly. Again, I hasten to add that youth was a great thing to have on our side back then. We would come out of the studio at lunchtime and none of us would even think of going back to the apartment for a sleep. We would have a big lunch, and off we would go for the afternoon and evening.'

The late Larry Gogan, one of RTÉ's most iconic presenters, would arrive at the studio at lunchtime and record the links for the programme. 'He was a fabulous guy, and many times we would wait to hear what he was saying in the links. He had a great broadcasting voice,' says Paddy. Larry would say, 'From Dublin, Ireland, it's The Capitol Showband,' and the listener knew instantly that the programme was aimed at an international audience.

There were some tunes on the programme that were 'seriously difficult to play', says Paddy, but there were also some humorous ones. One of those had the strange title of 'Yaka Hula Hicky Doola', which certainly didn't originate in Castleblayney. Or did it?

'I'm to blame for that tune being included,' laughs Paddy. 'One of the New Orleans jazz bands had a member named Bunk Johnston. He was a well-known trumpeter from the old school in New Orleans. He had retired and started a chicken farm when a recording company convinced him to make a comeback. He, along with another old-school clarinet player named George Lewis, suddenly became popular with all the young players in New Orleans. Before that, they would not have been allowed into a studio, because they were black, and that was incredibly sad and so wrong. Anyway, I had an old recording of "Yaka Hula Hicky Doola", and I convinced the band to do it.' It certainly illustrates how expansive a collection of rare jazz records Paddy's was. As stated in K-Tel's 'Butch Moore and The Capitol Showband – A Souvenir Programme': 'He is the proud possessor of an extensive library of vintage jazz records.'

'When we started playing "Yaka Hula Hicky Doola" for the dancers in the west of Ireland, they thought we had lost the run of ourselves. The dancers didn't care, and they thought it was a Hawaiian song, but it was a great Dixieland tune.'

A more serious piece of music that Paddy was instrumental in recording (pardon the pun!) was Irving Berlin's 'A Simple Melody', which was not at all simple to play. 'There were counter-harmonies in that number.

At the famous Preservation Hall, New Orleans, with members of the band.

Others would come in a bar after you and sing the same piece, and it worked out with the chords of the tune. It was all very intricate for us. But when we would look down at the crowds on the ballroom floors, the dancers couldn't care less. All them young fellas wanted to do was pick out a woman and get her out to dance.'

Paddy was praised by his bandleader Des Kelly for his clarinet solo on the track 'High Society' when Des introduced it on the album 'The Capitol Showband – A Collector's item': 'Paddy Cole's clarinet solo on that number always drew particular attention.' And not alone did it get praise from Des, but also from the host of the *Late Late Show*, Gay Byrne, a discerning connoisseur of jazz music.

'It was considered that if a clarinet player could play the solo in "High Society", then he was a good player,' says Paddy. 'I even remember my father saying to me when I was young, "Oh! When you can play the clarinet solo in 'High Society', I'll say you're a good one." Then when we had the reunion with The Capitol, and we were talking to Gay Byrne about our lives and the music that we played. He said, "What are ye going to play for us now?" and we replied, "High Society". Gay looked at me in a quizzical way and said, "Are you going to try that clarinet solo?" and I answered, "Yes, I am." Gay replied, "Well, I await with interest," as he walked across to his seat. Thanks be to God I played it without a fluff.'

The years 1964 and '65 probably saw The Capitol reach the pinnacle of their success. They achieved a series of firsts during those two years: They became the first Irish showband to record an album. They became the first Irish band to play Sunday Night at the Palladium in London, with 31 million viewers watching them on BBC TV. The band had its first number one in the Irish pop charts, and followed it up with two further number ones in a row. And lead singer Butch Moore became the first Irish representative in the Eurovision Song Contest.

But the dark clouds of change, and of possible missed international opportunities in both the US and the UK, were on the not-too-distant horizon. Personally, Paddy Cole was on cloud nine, as love and marriage were on the more immediate horizon for him.

Chapter 6

Marriage, Marquees and a Hurley in the Head!

Around the time that The Capitol were making inroads into the music scene in the UK, another Irish group, The Bachelors, were heading to the top of the charts there. Songs such as 'Charmaine' in 1962, 'Whispering' in 1963 and their number one UK hit 'Diane' in 1964 all helped the trio from Dublin become superstars in England. Their success helped The Capitol, not alone in the UK, but also in Germany, as Paddy recalls.

'The success of The Bachelors helped us in the UK for the simple reason that Phil Solomon was managing them as well as promoting us over there.

Apart from doing our own Sunday Night at the Palladium for BBC in 1965, we got other gigs there in 1964, such as midweek shows with The Bachelors. We even went to Germany and did tours there with The Bachelors. It was mostly air force bases that we played there. Phil Solomon organised all those trips. The Bachelors were huge international stars then, and it was great to work with them in Germany as well as in England.'

The Bachelors were comprised of Dublin brothers Con and Dec Cluskey and John Stokes. In 1964, they had more records in the UK charts than The Beatles. They also had top five hits in the USA with 'Dianne' and 'I Believe', as well as charting in many other countries around the world. So, the close association with The Bachelors certainly benefited The Capitol.

The popularity of The Capitol on the Irish dancing and recording scene was still growing apace, along with their international work. Paddy attributes a lot of their UK and Irish success to their weekly Radio Luxembourg show.

The Capitol were not augmented by any extra musicians when playing for those programmes. They simply gathered around the microphones and played the tracks live for each show, with none of the computer enhancements that can make almost everything sound perfect today. 'There were no session men on any of those tracks, just the band. In comparison to present-day recording facilities it was a bit archaic and primitive back then,' said Des Kelly in the sleeve notes of 'The Capitol Showband – A Collector's Item'.

Paddy says that going in to record the first ever Irish showband album was 'just another day's work'. There was a lot of discussion in advance about what songs and tunes they should do, and they all had an input regarding selecting material. Paddy again recorded 'Lagan Love', and this time it got to be released. The vinyl album was titled *Presenting The Capitol Showband*.

'We tried to keep it a varied selection, and we tried to feature all the members of the band, as a way of displaying that the band was versatile. For example, the track "Silver Threads and Golden Needles" featured all the boys in the band. It was a song with lots of harmonies. Jimmy Hogan was very much to the fore on that track on mandolin.

'My own favourite track was "Angelina" a Louis Prima number, rooted in New Orleans jazz and swing. He was a great favourite of mine, and Don Long did a wonderful version of it on the album. His version was a showstopper any place we played. It was enjoyable to play, even though there was a tricky bit of playing in it for the brass section. Even during the reunion of The Capitol in the eighties, when Don did "Angelina", the places would go bananas! The fans all remembered him doing it from the early 1960s.

'Very few people, if anyone in showbands, would have been doing Louis Prima material back then. It wasn't really a dance number, but more for cabaret. But Don did such a magnificent version that it worked on all our shows and on the first album. In fact, it was Don who introduced me to the material of Louis Prima when I came to Dublin first.

'Paul Sweeney was still in the band when we recorded that debut album. When Paul left the band to go back to college, he didn't play live with us again until one of the reunion tours in the 1980s.'

Paddy's Dublin friend Vincent McBrierty supplied him with a lot of the New Orleans records that he listened to in Dublin. 'We are still friends to this day, and we still discuss some of those records right up to the present time. We often talk about the different New Orleans musicians, different clarinet players and their styles. Vincent is an excellent clarinet player himself, but just as a hobby.'

John Woods, the Irish chief of Pye Records in Dublin, had 'some input' into The Capitol getting their recording contract. Paddy says he wasn't even aware that another UK label, Delyse, was also involved. That is stated in the K-Tel booklet published for the reunion of The Capitol Showband in 1984: 'Isabella Wallich is General Manager of the label. She is a niece of the co-founder of the Gramophone industry, the late Fred Gaisbert.'

'It was news to me when that was revealed in the tour magazine, as it was John Woods in Dublin that we were working with on the album. The LP was successful because it was the first album by an Irish showband, and it sold well among the Irish in the UK also. We did all those recordings very quickly. I remember us going into the Eamon Andrews Studios with producer Fred O'Donovan. We all just stood there with the microphones in front of us and played and sang all the tracks. The whole project was completed in less than a day.

'Nowadays, people would spend weeks or even months doing an album. We just played and sang as if we were on stage. Everything was so new to us in the recording studio. There were no enhancements of any of the tracks and no session musicians. Now, they can enhance recordings and even in some instances if somebody is out of tune, they can tweak it up into tune. Even when I was doing the "King of the Swingers" album, decades later, we just went in and played it. There was no enhancement either, but we took longer to do that album than the first one with The Capitol.

'Back then with our first LP, we were pioneering something without realising it. Going into the studio and doing it all in a few hours was no big deal for us. It was remarkably like what we were doing for the Radio Luxembourg shows. We just went in and played and sang, and when it was recorded that was that. We just moved on to what needed to be done next.'

The album was not released in the USA, even during their tours over there. He does not remember them taking any copies of it to the live shows, either at home or abroad. 'The only copies we brought to the USA were probably promotional ones to give to radio stations. At that time, showbands never sold records or any other merchandise at live gigs. That all came later, when I was doing the cabaret scene, and it was also there for The Capitol reunion gigs.'

Meanwhile, after a dance in Newcastle West, County Limerick, in 1963, Paddy met someone who would have a profound influence on the rest of his life. 'A man from the Limerick area, who I knew from working in the bank in Castleblayney, was at the dance that night. He came up to say hello to me afterwards, and his girlfriend plus a few others, including Helen, were with him. He had given them a lift in his car to the dance, and he introduced me to them. I said hello and chatted with them for a while before they went away. Afterwards, I remarked to our drummer Johnny Kelly that there was one fabulous-looking girl in that group. I also said that I was sorry I didn't stay talking to her for longer.'

Probably thinking that he had missed his chance of getting to know her better, Paddy forgot about the incident. But as fate would have it, they were to meet on a Dublin street about a week later, on a Monday evening.

'I was with Johnny Kelly again, as a passenger in his VW car. Driving along Westmoreland Street in Dublin, I saw this same blond girl walking along the footpath. I shouted to Johnny, "Pull up, pull up quick!"

'I jumped out and went over to the girl and her friend. I said "hello", and the two of them stopped and replied "hello", and they gave me a dirty look. Then I said to Helen, "I met you in Newcastle West at a dance a week ago." She studied me for a moment and replied, "Oh! I remember you now, you were playing in the band." She introduced me to her friend Phena O'Boyle, and told me they were both students in Dublin. Phena later went on to become famous as a fish cookery advisor on TV with Bord Íasca Mhara (BIM), the Irish fish council.'

Paddy decided that he wasn't going to miss his chance to get to know Helen better this second time. 'I was going back to Castleblayney until the Friday of that week, as we were off from playing for a few nights. So, I was in like a rocket, asking her would she like to go to the Ags dance in Dublin on Wednesday night week. She replied that she would, and I asked where she was staying, as I would pick her up. She was staying in a hostel in Mountjoy Square and I arranged to collect her at the hostel at eight o'clock on the night of the dance.

'But alas, I was late leaving Castleblayney on the evening of the dance, and some incident also happened along the road back to Dublin that caused traffic delays. I didn't arrive in Dublin till after nine, and I knew I was in trouble. But I went around to the hostel anyway and at least registered the fact that I hadn't forgotten about it. After ringing the bell, a lady opened the door and I said that I was seeking to speak with Helen Hehir. "Excuse me," she replied, "she was here earlier, but she has gone to bed." The other woman knew that Helen had been waiting for someone to collect her at eight o'clock, and that she had been let down. So, this other lady cut the socks off me for not being there on time. I asked if she could give her a message, that I apologised, but I had got delayed along the way. At that stage, I was thinking to myself that this potential girlfriend is gone now.

'But then the other lady said, "Hold on a minute and I'll see if she is in bed." Then she came back and said, "Helen will be down in a minute, as she hadn't gone to bed." Then Helen arrived down, and accepted my genuine

Paddy and Helen on O'Connell Bridge, Dublin, 1962.

excuse and my apology. When I asked if she was still okay to go to the dance, she said yes. So things worked out well from such a shaky start!'

He says that even though she was from Limerick, and he was a travelling musician from Monaghan, their courtship worked well because they both lived in Dublin. 'We saw a lot of each other during the day as Helen was flexible, being in college, and I would arrange to meet her often at lunch time. We also met on nights that I was off from the band, and I started to stay more in Dublin and less in Castleblayney.'

The management of bands in those times always wanted to keep it quiet if young singers or musicians had girlfriends or if they were married. 'That was particularly true with lead singers. They would also knock a few years off your age in press releases for the newspapers. I found this out to my detriment once. It was on an occasion that I went home to Castleblayney and went into McAree's pub for a drink. Two or three lads that were in the same class as me in school started giving me a rough time about my fake age. It seems there was a story in the local paper about me, but the band's management had knocked three or four years off my age! The boys in 'Blayney weren't long letting me know what age I really was.'

In the Ireland of the early 1960s, big marquee tents in fields were becoming more popular for dance festivals, called carnivals. But for a time, The Capitol didn't play in them.

'At one stage, Des Kelly made a decision not to play in the marquees, as the sound quality wasn't great and some of the working conditions weren't either. But when the hurling club in Des's local area of Turloughmore had a marquee festival of dancing to raise funds for the club, we played that. Afterwards, we started to play more marquees, and I enjoyed them, especially on fine summer's evenings. The facilities, such as toilets and dressing rooms for bands, were very basic. It certainly wouldn't be acceptable nowadays. Sometimes lads might also jump over a fence and lift the edge of the canvas to slip into the dance for free.

'There is a famous story told in showbusiness circles about a time when promoter Jim Hand had international group The Tremeloes here on tour,' says Paddy. The Tremeloes were a major pop group in England around the same time as The Capitol were big stars here. The UK group had their first hit in 1963 with a cover version of 'Twist and Shout', a song by Bert Berns and a hit for The Isley Brothers. One of The Tremeloes' biggest hits was 'Silence is Golden' five years later.

'They were doing two gigs in Ireland on the one night. One was in a ballroom, and the other was at a marquee tent in the west of Ireland. There was a mad rush to get them there on time, and the marquee was packed to capacity when they arrived. So promoter Jim Hand thought that the quickest way to get them in was around the back of the tent and by lifting the canvas. But he hadn't told the committee about this, and it was a hurling club that was running that dance. They had members of the club, some with hurleys, deployed to stop people from getting in under the canvas for free.

The first member of The Tremeloes to get in under the canvas encountered one of the stewards, who thought he was someone trying to get in for free. He gave the pop star a wallop of a hurley across the back of the head. There was pandemonium, but the hurlers who were stewards at the marquee didn't give a fiddler's. They were not letting anyone in for free under the canvas. It was all eventually explained and as always, the show must go on, and it did.'

Paddy recalled another marquee story in an interview with Sean Creedon in *Ireland's Own* magazine in April 2020. It involved well-known Galway dance promoter and marquee company owner Frank Fahy: 'There had been a bad storm that day and the wind had caused the tent to collapse at one end. When we arrived, we saw Frank, who was a fine strong man, stripped to the waist, pulling ropes with other fellows to put it back up again. That continued for some time while we were unloading the band equipment. We all hoped that the tent would stay up for the rest of the night!'

Frank Fahy later established the Eventus company, which is hugely successful nowadays in providing modern marquees, mostly for corporate functions.

In that *Ireland's Own* story, Paddy also said there was often 'a bit of a discussion' afterwards at ballrooms and marquees about the fee. But in the early years with The Capitol, that was largely an issue for either the road manager or the band's manager.

'Our road manager was Sean Jordan, and Jim Doherty was the band's manager, and it was their task to make sure that we got the agreed fee. That was especially true if the band was booked on a percentage of the admission takings. It was important that the band "got as fair a crack of the whip as possible", so to speak.

'But it could be difficult to keep an eye on the numbers that were admitted. Later, lads would sometimes have clickers in their pockets to try and get an accurate number of the attendance. But in the heel of the hunt, you usually just settled for what seemed like a fair fee. As they would say around my home place in Monaghan when a football team wouldn't be doing well, "It's best to take your beating and move on."

Playing marquees for a parish committee could sometimes be a bit tricky. I experienced it with The Capitol and later with The Paddy Cole Band, when I was the bandleader. The hardest person to deal with was often the parish priest. When you went to him to get paid, he might at times put on a sob story about it not being as good a crowd as they had expected. Whether you were on a set fee or a percentage of the takings, you were going to take a hit anyway during such discussions. So the object of the exercise was not to take as big a hit as the promoter intended you to take. It was a bit of a cat-and-mouse exercise,' laughs Paddy. 'But I have very fond memories of those times, and we made great friends with committees and different people who were running carnivals.'

In those years of 1963 and '64, The Capitol had big competition, both in the charts and on the live dancing scene. Even in those pre-Hucklebuck days, Brendan Bowyer and The Royal Showband were at number one with 'Kiss Me Quick'. Dickie Rock and The Miami also had a chart topper with 'The Candy Store on the Corner'. But was it all friendly competition between the bands – or not?

'It was always friendly competition, but every showband wanted to be as big as possible,' says Paddy. 'The Royal Showband had the advantage over us, as they had started before us and were well established. The Royal Showband also had the first showband hit single, with Tom Dunphy singing 'Come Down the Mountain Katie Daly', which also gave them a head start over the rest.

'Our band, The Capitol, probably came along next, and were knocking at the door after The Royal. Dickie Rock and The Miami were, by coincidence, being managed by the same office as The Capitol. We only found out afterwards that in the early days of The Miami, the office was selling their dates along with those of The Capitol – to get a date with The Capitol, a ballroom or marquee promoter might also have to take the other band for a few dates as well. I suppose it was good business to get a band launched.

'Another big showband was Eileen Reid and The Cadets, and they were managed by a true gentleman named Tom Costello. He went on to launch and manage folk star Johnny McEvoy for many years. Tom was a native of Mayo, and he only died recently at a big age. He got on well with our management, but in general all the managements got on well. Some of them would contact each other from time to time about carnivals that had dance dates available. They might tell our management, or vice versa, that there were a few free dates there and give them the phone contact to ring for a possible gig. They would play ball businesswise generally, and there was good cooperation,' says Paddy.

The Capitol Showband hit the number one spot in the Irish charts for the first time in December 1964, with 'Down Came the Rain', with Butch Moore on vocals. It was to be the first of a three-in-a-row of number ones for the band. But while Paddy says the first number one was a huge boost for the band, he hasn't much recollection of how the song happened to be selected by them.

'It was a lovely, slow ballad and I think it must have been Butch who selected it, as he was the lead vocalist. Butch had a habit of slapping his right thigh with his hand beating out the time. He was a handsome-looking guy and the girls loved that song, even though it was a slow ballad at a time when many of the number ones were up-tempo songs.'

The other two number ones in the trio for The Capitol came in March and April of the following year, 1965. 'Born to Be With You' topped the Irish hit parade in March, and the Eurovision song sung by Butch, 'Walking the Streets in the Rain', was number one in April.

As 1964 morphed into 1965, Paddy was about to have one of the busiest years of his life. He and Helen had got engaged in 1964, and had their marriage all planned for 27 February 1965. But they had no idea how quickly The Capitol would rocket to the top in the spring of 1965, and how busy they would be. None of the band, or indeed the management, had a clue in 1964 about their upcoming involvement in the 1965 Eurovision or Sunday Night at the Palladium.

'In fact, we had to cut short our honeymoon after I got a phone call to the hotel where we were staying. It was from the band, saying they had to do two TV shows in London, "The Eamon Andrews Show" and "Thank Your Lucky Stars". So we had to cut our honeymoon short by four or five days and fly back to London,' says Paddy.

Paddy and Helen stayed in the Cumberland hotel, where a prank was played on them by the hotel manager. Paddy wasn't aware that his friend, Ignatius Murray, was managing the London hotel.

'We got a phone call to our room from the hotel reception, and this guy with a Cockney accent said, "Mr Cole, we have a complaint here about you. We have been told that you brought a young lady into your bedroom last night." I reared up on the fellow with the Cockney accent on the phone, and said, "Yes, of course I've got a young woman in the room with me – she is my wife." He replied, "Oh! We have heard that sort of an excuse before." I was so vexed that I was about to go down to the reception and have it out with him, when Murray said in his Donegal accent, "How ya doin', scout?" I could have killed him,' laughs Paddy.

'It was so hectic during those early months of 1965 for us with the band, but it must have been more hectic for the management, rearranging many of our live dates. The Eurovision Song Contest and the "Sunday Night at the Palladium" TV show came down on us all like a sheet of lightning. The management had to rearrange dates at home and cancel some other dates. They had to make time available for Butch to practise too, as he was the first person to represent Ireland in the Eurovision Song Contest. It was such a big deal in those days. When he came back to Dublin Airport, there were thousands of people there to greet him. That was the case with other Irish singers in the following years also. Then, of course, "Sunday Night at the Palladium" was a huge appearance for us to be preparing for as well.'

Those years were a time of great joy for Paddy's parents as well. They saw their son getting married and his band scaling new heights on the music scene. His dad took an interest in the way he was playing tunes, both live and on record. 'I always had great admiration for him,' says Paddy, 'because with truly little resources, he was trading in saxophones, he was bringing jazz records in from the States and he was big into photography. I remember him having an old Kodak camera that he could even take selfies with. He had some sort of a delayed action switch attached to it that allowed him to run back into the picture. He was a man before his time. Thank God both my mother and father lived through this success and those great times with The Capitol.

'Even afterwards, in The Paddy Cole Band times, I used to do a Monday night session in the hotel in Castleblayney and my mother would come along with some of my sisters. I would join up with some local musicians, including my brother-in-law Ronnie Duffy from Big Tom's band. We have very fond memories of those sessions and how much my mother loved this. She saw more of the success than my dad, as he died before her. But he also saw a lot of it and was immensely proud of it.

'Later, with The Paddy Cole Band, promoter Tony Loughman took an All-Stars Showbusiness football team to New York, and it was a joy for

SUNDAY NIGHT AT THE LONDON PALLADIUM

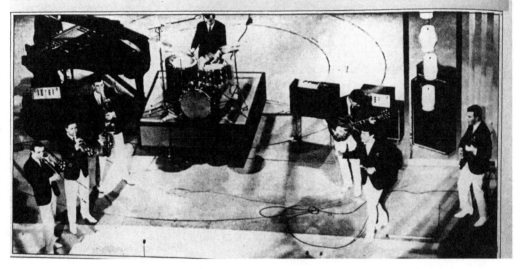

The Capitol Showband on stage, Sunday Night at the London Palladium.

Helen and myself to take my dad along. My mother wouldn't travel, but my father came. He shared a room with the famous footballer Liam Maguire, who had won the All-Ireland with Cavan. He was later Sergeant Liam Maguire and became great friends with my father.

'My father always gave me good advice when I first started drinking during my time with The Capitol. He would tell me, "Never drink before you go on stage. You will think that you are playing well, but everyone watching will know that you are not." Those were wise words indeed, and they resonated with me years later in Las Vegas, when we would be doing three shows per night, six nights a week. My father's advice stuck in my mind and I always just went to the coffee shop before the shows. I might have a few beers after the last show, but would never drink before playing.'

Chapter 7

The Highs and Lows of International Success

T he good times continued to roll for Paddy Cole and The Capitol in 1965, the biggest year of all for the band. An appearance on 'Sunday Night at the Palladium' in London was watched by over 30 million TV viewers, and the band had two number one records in two months. Shortly afterwards, Butch Moore became the first ever Irish representative in the Eurovision Song Contest. Offers of coast-to-coast tours in the US and nationwide tours in the UK came their way, but were not accepted, mainly due to the band's popularity at home.

But within a year, the wheels were coming off the showband wagon, not alone for The Capitol, but for all showbands in Ireland. The bands tried to adapt, but the ballad boom, fuelled by ceremonies marking the fiftieth anniversary of the 1916 Rising, spawned new stars such as The Dubliners, The Ludlows, The Johnstons, Johnny McEvoy, Danny Doyle and, later, The Wolfe Tones and Emmet Spiceland. The Irish songs topping the pop charts in 1966 reflected the shifting sands. According to *The Larry Gogan Book of Irish Chart Hits* (Maxwell Publishing, 1987), six of the nine number ones by Irish artists that year were ballads.

But before this seismic shift for the Irish music scene, The Capitol scaled heights never achieved before by any showband. Paddy says he will never forget their appearance on the iconic 'Sunday Night at the Palladium' TV programme on BBC, with its enormous audience. Even the death of one of England's most iconic politicians didn't scuttle the show, only suspending the screening of their performance until the following Sunday.

'We knew it was a huge opportunity for the band, and of course we decided to give it our best shot. We were all 100 per cent behind it, but on reflection, perhaps we didn't capitalise enough on it. Shortly afterwards, we were offered a six-month residency stint for six nights a week in the Palladium. Logistically, it wasn't suitable for us, because we had already confirmed so many dance dates at home. Also, as some of the lads were married, it wasn't suitable for them. We would be flying home from London late every Saturday night or early Sunday morning, just to spend Sunday back in Dublin. Then we would have to fly back to London early every Monday to play the Palladium again that night. For all those reasons, we decided not to accept the offer. At that time, the London Palladium was packed for shows six nights a week.

'On reflection, it would have looked well on our CV to have the words "Direct from the London Palladium". But it was only afterwards that this crossed our minds. We took into consideration that some of the boys were married with children. It would be unfair on them to take on that contract. It could also cause lads to leave our band to work with other bands back home.

'I know that promoter Phil Solomon was unhappy about our decision. He felt it would lead to a big breakthrough for us in the UK. But there again, Phil Solomon was probably thinking of Phil Solomon and having another act to sell "direct from The London Palladium". He had plans for us to be working in top night clubs all over England and Scotland as well as in Germany. While it might have made us into a real international act, it just wasn't suitable for all of us to be working so much of the time abroad.'

On the night of the show, the excitement was palpable for the boys in the band as they waited for their curtain call. Standing nervously back-stage, they were slightly irked by the lengthy, and somewhat corny, intro-duction by Norman Vaughan. He was a comedian as well as the regular presenter of the show at the time. Norman was well known for doing the Cadbury's Roses chocolates TV advert with the slogan 'Roses grow on you'. He introduced many famous people on 'Sunday Night at the Palladium', including Frank Sinatra, Judy Garland, Tommy Cooper and, in January 1965, The Capitol Showband.

'Norman's introduction was, "Now we have a crowd of Irish guys next and we have been walking them around the block for the past hour to sober them up." While I was kind of pissed off with that remark, it was also when Bram McCarthy whispered something into my ear that scared the wits out of me. Bram said, "If that curtain doesn't go up in the next three seconds I'm out of here." I was thinking to myself, if he does a runner, how am I going to cover for his trumpet parts with my sax? Luckily for everyone, the curtain went up and we all went straight into playing.

'Earlier, at rehearsals, we recognised some of the top musicians in England who were in the pit orchestra. They included Kenny Baker on trumpet, Don Lusher on trombone and others. They were chuffed that we recognised them, but Bram was somewhat worried about playing in front of those musicians. In a lovely gesture after rehearsals, Kenny Baker came around to our dressing room and put him at ease. He was famous for the Kenny Baker Dozen and later the Kenny Baker six-piece band. He was a brilliant player and he came to our dressing room simply to help Bram relax. He said that, from what he heard at rehearsals, Bram was a first-class player. Kenny said something like, "We are down in the orchestra pit doing our gig; ye are doing your gig up on stage. But we could not go up there and do what you guys are doing with only eight players." It was a great confidence boost for Bram, and really relaxed him. He was a brilliant player anyway and a perfectionist. But what a lovely gesture from a famous player such as Kenny Baker. Sometimes other professionals, and resident bands, would try to roast you and make life harder for you.'

The night The Capitol played at the London Palladium, Winston Churchill died, but their show still went on before a packed audience. However, the TV broadcast of it was held over until the following Sunday night.

'I'll always remember that it was 24 January 1965, but I don't know if it was our playing at the London Palladium that pushed Sir Winston over the top. He might have thought that this was more than he could take.' So laughed Paddy on *Des's Island Discs* on RTÉ Radio 1 with Des Cahill on 31 March 2020.

All BBC TV shows were postponed that night, as all programming was dedicated to the life and times of Churchill. When it was screened on the following Sunday night, Paddy watched it far from the spotlights of the Palladium, on a tiny TV set back in the southeast of Ireland.

'We were playing at a dance in Wexford, and we saw it on a snowy screen on a black-and-white TV in a hotel there. It was good to see it, even if it meant little to Irish TV viewers. It didn't benefit us much in Ireland, because most people couldn't get BBC TV reception, only those along the east coast. It got good publicity though, especially in the newspapers, with many of them reporting on our performance at the Palladium. But "so what?" is how most Irish dancers looked at it. To them it was just another gig, as they didn't realise that this was *the* big gig in the UK to be doing.'

Even though The Capitol didn't accept the six-month contract at the Palladium, they were invited back for several other shows there, including one with Roy Orbison. 'He had his band over from the US, and when singing "Pretty Woman", I can still picture in my mind the band having two drummers to lay down that four-to-the-bar beat. We were watching backstage, and he had one of the drummers behind the curtain, just playing four-to-the-bar. The other drummer was visible on the stage. We were at the side, making faces at the guy behind the curtain, trying to make him laugh, but he was fully focussed. My own thoughts were, wouldn't it be more spectacular to show the audience the two drummers on stage?'

Soon after their Sunday Night at the Palladium appearance, The Capitol recorded a new single in London. It was to be the second of their three-in-a-row number one hits: 'Born To Be With You'.

'Phil Coulter arranged and produced it. He put extra emphasis again on the use of the baritone sax, as he felt it gave a great depth to the song.

So much so that even to this day when you hear it, at the very end, you will hear how he let the baritone sax low note ring out exceptionally long. It rings out for even a split second after everything else on the backing had finished. He did a great job on that recording,' says Paddy.

His views seem to be borne out in an article in the reunion booklet for Butch Moore and Capitol Showband published in 1984. 'The result was a vibrant and refreshing treatment of one of the band's best recordings.'

Looking back on that recording now, Paddy says there was no time wasted while they were in London, or in getting back to gigging when they came home afterwards. 'The spare time we had over there was used to go into the studio, where Phil Coulter was working, and record that single. We had extraordinarily little time off when I think of it now. We didn't care back then, but at my stage in the game now, it would be different. If somebody had me playing in London one night, recording there the next day and a gig back in Ireland the next night, I would say you are joking. I might even use stronger words,' laughs Paddy. 'But in those days, we just did it, and as I have said before, youth was on our side.'

The band were soon back in London again, for an appearance on ITV's *Thank Your Lucky Stars*. As was usual back then, everything was played live. 'There were no backing tracks in those days. Nowadays artists can appear on many of the top TV shows with a backing track and just mime or sing to it. But we went in and played on *Thank Your Lucky Stars*, and you had to get it right – there was no safety net. We got nice compliments after that TV show from the producers and the floor crew, who said they were bowled over by our live performance. It was nice to hear that, and without sounding like I'm blowing my own trumpet – or sax! – it proved all the band were top-class players.'

After leaving the bright lights and adulation on the set of a UK TV show, it was home to the daily and nightly grind of gigs for The Capitol. They would assemble at The Belvedere Hotel in Dublin around midday most days to board their bus for the dance that night. 'We had as much comfort as possible on the road in our customised bus, but we still had to do the journey. In those days, there wasn't the roads infrastructure in Ireland that there is now. Our bus was comfortable, but slow, as there was a heavy load of equipment on it, plus all of us. We did the journeys with our road manager Sean Jordan, affectionately known as "the spoofer", at the wheel. If we were going to Donegal for example, the saving grace was that we might have a booking in Sligo the following night. If so, we had the luxury of being able to stay in a hotel. But, after the highs of the TV shows in England, it was still back to porridge, back to basics, back home.'

In the middle of all of their success in the UK, Paddy and Helen got married in Dublin, on 27 February 1965. 'I remember rushing back from a gig in Carlow the night before the wedding. All the boys and I high-tailed it back as quickly as possible to Dublin that night. They were all there the next day in the church, and at the reception in the Country Club in Portmarnock. Helen and I headed off afterwards to Marbella for our honeymoon. But, of course, we had to cut that short for the band's appearance on TV in London.'

In the middle of those busy times, The Capitol's lead singer, Butch Moore, was selected to sing for Ireland as the country's first representative in the Eurovision Song Contest. 'It was great, but also a headache for management, as a lot of dates had to be cancelled while Butch was away in Naples. We watched him on TV back home, and he did Ireland proud, finishing in a very creditable sixth place. This was an era when good singers such as Butch were representing countries. Nowadays, to be honest, I cringe when I see some of the acts, including some of the strange ones we sent out over the years – 'nuff said! But the ballroom owners weren't too impressed back then when they were told The Capitol weren't available for a gig because Butch was in Naples.

'Even if there was a lot of rearranging of schedules, it was worth it all. There were thousands at the airport to welcome him home, and when we stayed in the Metropole Hotel in Cork shortly afterwards, there were 1,000 people lined up outside on the street on a Sunday morning. They just wanted to get a glimpse of Butch. Fair play to him, he went out and thanked them and waved to them. Meanwhile, we were spirited out through the kitchens to the back door, where our bus was waiting. That's how big the Eurovision was back then.'

Butch's song, 'Walking the Streets in the Rain', gave The Capitol their third number one in a row in the Irish charts.

Across the Atlantic, new opportunities were opening up for The Capitol. They were still huge among the Irish in the ballrooms over there, but after playing a gig with a difference for students in Villanova University, other work beckoned. A promoter named Jimmy Barker, whose father came from Monaghan, booked them for the university gig.

'We thought it would be a tough concert for us, before an audience of students. But we did all the old rock'n'roll hits, plus the ballads, and they loved it. Another promoter heard about this and he wanted us to do a coast-to-coast tour of college campuses in America. It would have taken six months, but again, after discussing it, we decided it would be too long to be away from home and the Irish scene. It would have meant cancelling a lot of work at home, while only benefiting us before a new and different audience in America. But perhaps we underestimated just how huge that potential audience was. We didn't do it, but the folk group The Irish Rovers did. They ended up being a huge group for years after that.' In the summer of 1968, The Irish Rovers had a massive international hit with 'The Unicorn', and they were contracted to the major US record label MCA.

'They were living in Canada, so it suited them better than us to accept the US universities tour. They went on to do many tours of the American college campus scene, and in Canada as well. I was told afterwards by members of the group that the college campus tours in the States were massive for them. That could have been The Capitol – but such is life,' says Paddy philosophically. 'We were pioneering stuff that we didn't realise we were doing at the time. But to be honest, we just didn't want to be travelling for six months, from one side of the US to the other.'

Meanwhile, in Ireland, the music scene was changing, as the ballad boom became the latest craze. In the years 1966 and 1967, Irish ballads dominated the charts. It started in January of '66, when Larry Cunningham modernised an Irish *sean nós*-style song that his mother sang, titled 'Lovely Leitrim'. It was written by an old boyfriend of hers, Philip Fitzpatrick, before he emigrated to the USA, where he became a police officer in New York. Sadly, Fitzpatrick was shot on duty, 'while bravely trying to prevent an armed robbery and died in hospital on 26 May 1947'. (*Spring* police magazine, June 1947, New York Publications) So, he never heard his ballad being sung by Larry and The Mighty Avons.

This was the first of six ballads to top the Irish pop charts in 1966. The others were 'The Sea Around Us' by The Ludlows, 'The Black and Tan Gun' by Pat Smith and The Johnny Flynn Showband, 'Travelling People' by The Johnstons, 'Merry Ploughboy' by Dermot O'Brien and 'Muirsheen Durkin' by Johnny McEvoy.

PADDY COLE

As the 1966 commemorations for the Easter Rising cranked up, more rebel ballads made the charts. The showbands started to scramble for survival in this changed music scene by releasing ballads. In 1967 The Capitol, featuring drummer Johnny Kelly, had a number one with the ballad 'Black Velvet Band'. Also in the first month of 1967, Paddy Cole's school pal Big Tom McBride and The Mainliners had a massive hit with their countrified ballad 'Gentle Mother'.

The ballad boom didn't have great longevity, but it was the beginning of the end of the showband scene. Another new trend was singing pubs, with small groups playing and usually with no admission charge. This also contributed to the demise of the 'dry' dancehalls, which only had mineral bars and admission charges.

Ireland was changing economically, educationally, culturally and religiously in the mid- to late 1960s. Free education and free school transport, introduced by Minister Donogh O'Malley, was a game changer for many young rural people. Across the ocean, on the 'streets of San Francisco', free love and flower power was in vogue. Scott McKenzie's song about this was a number one in Ireland too – a chameleon country was emerging. Fame can be a fickle and fleeting thing, especially when music tastes change, and change was everywhere in the mid-'60s. Change hit The Capitol too, with the bombshell news that Butch Moore was leaving.

'It was a shock, but it was all very friendly and amicable. There was no animosity when Butch explained to us that a promoter had made him an offer he couldn't refuse. He was to be signed up to be the opening act in The Talk of the Town, the biggest club in London at that time. He was also promised a contract to work all the major clubs in England. All we could do was wish him well. He was such a lovely guy that we had farewell parties and all that for him.

'But the sad thing about it was that none of those things happened for him. He had been spoofed a bit by the promoter, and those gigs in the top UK clubs never materialised. But, as he said to us, if he didn't take the chance and try it, he would spend the rest of his life wondering why he didn't do so. It looked attractive to him, and the possibility was that maybe he could make it big in Britain. Butch was just a nice guy, but gullible to listen to that promoter. But it's all part and parcel of the experiences of life. Subsequently, the late Butch and his second wife Maeve Mulvany went on to become hugely popular singers in the States on the Irish pub and cabaret circuit.'

In his book *Tell Roy Rogers I'm Not In*, Tim Ryan summed up succinctly how the split hit both Butch and the band. 'Butch finally left The Capitol in the summer of '66, signalling the end of an era. The move fell flat for Moore, but it had major consequences for those he left behind.'

The band continued with Des Kelly, having a number three song in the Irish charts with 'The Streets of Baltimore'. Shortly afterwards, his brother Johnny hit the number one spot with 'Black Velvet Band', with the version by The Dubliners peaking at number four.

Looking back on it now, Paddy Cole is in no doubt that the parting of the ways for Butch and for The Capitol was a defining moment for both the singer and the band. 'But, and I must use the word but, despite the two hits by the Kelly brothers, once the lead singer moved on from any showband it changed everything. We had three new lead singers in the following years, and while they were all great singers, the dancers were still looking for Butch Moore and The Capitol. We had a young guy named Noel McNeill, then Tony O'Leary and later John Drummond. They were all fantastic artists.

'It was Phil Coulter who recommended John Drummond. He was from Scotland and was doing all the demo work for Phil in London. Subsequently he became a member of the RTÉ Orchestra. Tony O'Leary was a great singer. He was a finalist in the National Song Contest the year that Dana won it, when she went on to win the Eurovision. Noel McNeill was a real rocker and a great man on stage. He was good-looking and a real rock'n'roll kid. But they were all on a hiding to nothing, because people would always compare them to Butch. That happened with a lot of other bands when their lead singers left. The new man or woman, selected to replace the original lead singer, had the toughest gig of all time.'

Around this time other members of The Capitol also started to leave the band. Des and Johnny Kelly moved on to go into management of country bands. Des also launched the Ruby record label. It spawned recording stars such as Christy Moore and Planxty, Margo, The Smokey Mountain Ramblers, Dermot Henry and many more. When he left The Capitol, which he had been a co-founder of, Des realised that the writing was on the wall for the band.

On the CD *The Capitol Showband – A Collector's Item*, Des introduces the tracks, and he looks back upon a Paddy Cole recording as a possible hit that was missed. 'The song "Bottle of Wine", featuring Paddy on vocals, didn't get enough promotion to be a hit. But it came at a time when The Capitol's fame was fading fast. That was done towards the end of The Capitol days after Butch had left the band. I thought it should be included on this CD because it was a record that never got a proper chance.'

It eventually came to pass that Paddy was the only original member left in The Capitol. It was a case of last man out put out the lights, which he did in 1971. 'While Bram was also there from the early band, I was the only original member left at that time. Bram and I had to make a decision, because the crowds had dwindled so much that it was time to wind it all up. We made the decision one night in Killarney, when the band was due to go on two weeks' holiday. We paid the band members their holiday money out of what we had got for the gigs that weekend. Bram and I had little left, if anything at all, for ourselves. We said there was a need for time to think, and to talk all this over.'

To paraphrase the title of a hit song by The Seekers, the carnival really was over for The Capitol. But amazingly, during this time of turmoil in his life, Paddy got a phone call to see if he would join a new band being formed, called The Big 8. The band would include two of the most established names on the showband scene, Brendan Bowyer and Tom Dunphy of The Royal. They were already working for several months every year in Las Vegas with The Royal.

Paddy was initially somewhat sceptical about the offer. This was because a year earlier there had been similar soundings made to him about Brendan starting another band. But that never happened. 'The first one didn't come to anything because Brendan decided not to leave. It was only a sort of a feeler call that I got at that time. On that occasion, I just said to them, let me know if anything is happening. The next thing I heard was that Brendan was staying with The Royal. But I don't think the boys in The Royal were happy with the way things were going, and it was never the same after that.

'Then I got the second phone call, to see if I would join Brendan and Tom as bandleader, and to help them pick the new band members. They still had the contract to work six months of the year in Las Vegas, just as they had been doing with The Royal. So, with the demise the showband scene in Ireland, as country bands were taking over, and the end of The Capitol, it would be a no-brainer for me to take the offer. Helen and I had a chat about it, as we always did about all business decisions in our life. We agreed that it was a good opportunity, and I went ahead and told Brendan and Tom that I would join.

'Among the people I selected to join the new band was Twink [Adele King] as female vocalist. Jimmy Conway had been in another band with her and he was picked too. So also was Mickey O'Neill on drums, who had worked with me before. Brendan and Tom picked Dave Coady from Waterford, who was a trumpet player and a fabulous singer. He had been in the group The Real McCoy. Michael Keane from the Johnny McEvoy band came in on keyboards.

'They held some auditions for the band at the Old Shieling hotel in Dublin. Those were organised by promoter Bill Fuller, and while I felt uncomfortable, auditioning musicians that I knew, it was part of the job. We were off to a flying start with Brendan and Tom as the lead singers. Add to this the talent of Twink, plus the other great musicians and TJ Byrne as manager, and it looked good.'

Chapter 8

Vegas – City of Saints, Sinners and Mafia

'Sin City' is the most common nickname for Las Vegas, but it is also known as the 'entertainment capital of the world' and as the 'gambling capital of the world'. To this city of divergent attractions, from its sleazy underbelly to its high society, Paddy Cole went to play 'High Society' with the Big 8 in 1971.

'We did tours all over America at the Irish centres in places such as New York, Boston, Chicago and San Francisco, but Las Vegas was different. It was hard work too, as we were doing three shows a night, six nights a week, and each show was an hour long,' says Paddy.

The musicians went in advance to sort out accommodation, before the wives and families followed. 'We were told by management that this was the normal procedure, and so we all flew out first for a few weeks to get everything organised. We signed contracts for apartments, as close to the entertainment strip as possible.

'This was my first trip to Vegas, and in those days, the planes coming in flew low along the strip and it was a spectacular sight to see. Everybody on the plane was looking out the windows at this amazing line of lights below.'

The accommodation they found was excellent. 'It was in an apartment block called the Bali Hai. It was nicely situated, with a beautiful green area, tennis courts and swimming pools. During the day it was nice accommodation to relax in, especially when the kids were young. It was within walking distance of the Stardust, where we were playing.'

But walking to work in the heat of Las Vegas wasn't an option for Paddy or his colleagues. 'It was so warm there that we needed an old banger of a car with an air-cooling system. Otherwise we would be wrecked walking in the heat.'

One of Paddy's band colleagues, Twink, loved to take the two young Cole boys swimming. She was proud years later when hearing that they were winning awards for swimming. 'She always talks about teaching our kids to swim. She was proud as punch on hearing that Pearse, Pat and our daughter Karen who was born later, went on to swim with the Armagh club and represented Ulster.'

Paddy, Helen and family settled into life in Las Vegas, and the new-look band also settled quickly into the routine of performing in the Stardust Club. 'There is no doubt but that Brendan, Tom and The Royal Showband had ploughed the furrow there before us. Some of the die-hard fans of The Royal, who were residents there, would be asking us how members of The Royal were doing back home. They might say, "How is Eddie Sullivan?" or, "Do you ever see Michael Coppinger?" or, "How is Gerry Cullen?" It was nice that they remembered them.

'But it was a transient population in Vegas. We might get to know our audience before going to Ireland for the few months, but none of them would be there when we got back to Vegas. A lot of people at our gigs might be in Vegas for a few days' visit. If they were Irish, or Irish-American from anywhere in the States, they would gravitate to where the Irish band was playing. In fairness the gig would be packed every night, as it was for The Royal in the years before that.'

Getting a residency in a top club in Vegas was quite an achievement for any Irish band. It was almost impossible for outside musicians to get work there, due to the strength of the American Federation of Musicians union. That is where iconic Irish entrepreneur and promoter Bill Fuller, then living in Vegas, was a big influence for The Big 8. Bill was a larger-than-life character, who owned ballrooms and hotels in Ireland, England and the USA. This Kerry emigrant first became wealthy in the construction industry in the UK. His business empire ranged from ballrooms and rock venues in New York and London to gold mines in Las Vegas.

Bill Fuller died in the summer of 2008 at the age of ninety-one. He gained notoriety in his later years for having bankrolled bail, to the tune of over two million dollars, for a stripper in a high-profile murder case in Las Vegas. A story in the *Guardian* newspaper quoted him as saying that he 'was simply drawn to the case of Sandy Murphy by her surname and an absolute conviction that she was innocent'.

But in another story in the *Sunday Independent* in 2008, Liam Collins noted that a Dublin promoter had claimed that Bill 'was a mate of the mafia' in Las Vegas. However, Paddy Cole is more circumspect in his views regarding Bill Fuller's connections in Las Vegas. 'There is no doubt about it but the mafia controlled Vegas. There was a book written about it, an exposé on the mafia's control of Las Vegas, called *The Green Felt Jungle* – the "green felt" meaning the gambling tables. If some of the bosses in Vegas knew you even had that book, let alone that you were reading it, you would be gone straight away. It was exposing some people that we saw as upstanding citizens and bosses in the hotels, claiming they had been involved in shootings and robberies and other crimes.

'I can only speak for The Stardust where we worked; the bosses there were always genuinely nice to us. At times when we might be walking through the casino, which was twice as big as Croke Park, the bosses there might see us, and they would shout, "How ya doin', Irish?" They seemed to appreciate what we were doing there. But we heard that some of those bosses were notorious in their younger days. I never knew anything about Bill Fuller having mafia links. But I was aware that he could placate the American Federation of Musicians, so that we had no issues playing there. Bill Fuller was a very shrewd businessman. He built up a whole empire of ballrooms, bars, hotels and restaurants, all over Ireland and America.'

Elvis Presley came to see The Big 8 performing at their residency in The Stardust. Paddy vividly remembers meeting with 'The King' in his dressing room in Vegas. 'When we were taken through all the security checks to his dressing room, it was full of fitness equipment. It had rowing machines, weights, exercise bicycles, and all that sort of stuff. Elvis was a very fit man,

Ground breaking ceremony for the MGM Hotel, Las Vegas. Cary Grant and Raquel Welch, surrounded by showband performers and Irish dancers.

and what really impressed me was how tall he was. He was also a nice guy, humble and so friendly and pleased to meet us. Elvis was delighted too that Brendan was doing a tribute to him.'

It has been said that on hearing Brendan sing 'You Gave Me a Mountain', Elvis then decided to also record the song. Elvis attended The Big 8's show in The Stardust in disguise, but he let them know he was there in the strangest way. Paddy recalls the weird encounter: 'This man walked up to the stage, and of course his back was to the audience. The stage was a circular bandstand, and Brendan was down on his knees, singing "One Night With You". The man walking towards him was wearing a cloak and a hat, something like the Don character on the label of a bottle of Sandeman port. He tapped Brendan on the shoulder with a cane and when Brendan looked up, he recognised Elvis. Then Elvis turned and walked away out through a side door. When Brendan said as he finished the song, "That was Elvis," everybody laughed and applauded. But they didn't believe it – they thought it was just part of the act.'

Paddy says that it was a daring act for Elvis to carry out, even if he was disguised. But he probably had security guards placed all around the venue, and the management must have known about it in advance.

The Big 8 were impressed with the tight security Elvis had around his dressing room. 'It was the first time ever that I saw walkie-talkies being used. We had to go through door after door, and the security men would say to their colleagues, "The Irish guys are coming through." Then the door would open, and we would walk along another corridor to the next door, with the same procedure. It was amazing to see how his security personnel worked.'

Paddy saw a nasty side to one of the security crew on another occasion, a side that went unnoticed by Elvis that night. 'We were at the closing night of Liza Minnelli's show, and Elvis was in a circular booth, with security guards around him. The two booths beside him were also filled with his security guards. It was nice of him to stand up with all the others when Liza got a standing ovation. But before she came back for the encore, Elvis had gone. This was so that she would get all the attention at the end of her show. If Elvis was still there, he knew he would be a distraction – he was a true professional.

As he was leaving, with security in front of and behind him, an elderly man tried to reach out with his hand towards Elvis. The star was moving so quickly that he didn't even see him, but one of the security guards did, and gave him a karate chop on the arm. I was disgusted; I felt that it was totally uncalled for. It was simply one security guard trying to justify himself being there. Elvis never even saw the incident, as he was moving away so fast.'

Later, towards the end of his career, when Elvis had become very over-weight, Paddy watched him perform again. He felt sorry for the way Elvis was being manipulated and marketed simply as a product to make money for others. But he was full of admiration for the care given to Elvis by a local physician when he played Vegas.

'His physician in Vegas was a Dr Ghanem. We knew him well, as my wife was friendly with his secretary, Penny Pennington. The doctor would always be at the side of the stage, in case anything happened to Elvis when, sadly, he was so out of shape and overweight. When Elvis finished his stint in Vegas, he would give Dr Ghanem a present and it was always the choice of a car. This was the first time I heard the word "import" used regarding a car. Dr Ghanem would always pick an "import" car – maybe a Mercedes or a Jaguar, or something like that.

'One day when Elvis was in the doctor's clinic, he was chatting to Penny and she remarked that he was wearing a beautiful ring. Elvis said that he bought it when they were on tour in another part of the States. They exchanged a few more words, and that was the end of their conversation. But after he left, there was an envelope with her name on it left at reception in the clinic. When she opened it, the ring was in the envelope as a gift to her. At that time, in the early 1970s, it was worth about $5,000, which would have bought two houses for me where I came from,' roars Paddy.

Paddy has only one regret about the Big 8's meeting with Elvis. It is that nobody thought to bring along a camera – there are no photographs of their meeting with this true music icon.

Seeing Frank Sinatra in concert was another highlight of Paddy's time in Las Vegas, and a triply enjoyable experience for him. This is because there was such a doubt about whether Sinatra would show up that night that Caesar's Palace had booked two other acts also. 'Sinatra was in dispute with Caesar's Palace at the time, and he hadn't shown up for his previous engagement there. The place was closed for a week, which was a terrible financial hit for the venue. Their object was to put on those big stars, get the people inside and then fleece them at the gambling tables.

'For example, when Willie Nelson and Waylon Jennings appeared there, all the Texas oil barons followed them. The bosses of the venues were smiling from ear to ear, because these guys would be spending millions and not worrying about it. But when Caesar's Palace were unsure whether Sinatra would show for the concert, they also booked The Count Basie Band and Ella Fitzgerald for safety. You can imagine what an amazing concert that was!'

Paddy says that he was flabbergasted at the vast sums of money people would squander at the gambling tables in Las Vegas. He says that it probably seemed less to those placing the bets, because what they were putting down were plastic chips instead of cash.

'If they had to count out $1,000 in notes, they might not put on the bets as quickly. But when the gambler was throwing down a chip representing the sum, it looked different. So, they went to the bank and changed their dollars into chips. After a gig, we might see a big crowd around a table, and we knew there was a "high roller" at that table. I remember watching one high roller putting down his chips, and Helen asked me how much those chips were worth. I said that every bet he was putting down would easily buy two houses back in Dublin. That guy was there for hours doing this, and of course the bosses would love that. Suffice to say that the gambling house always won.'

Of course, Vegas was about more than just gambling and music. It had dancers that were very different to any Paddy would have seen in the small parish halls of Ireland! Sometimes 'The Bare Touch of Vegas', a group of girls wearing nothing but a smile, would put on their show either before or after The Big 8's performance. Paddy says they were nice girls, but it was 'a far cry from playing in Moate ballroom' – probably too cold in Moate!

'When walking along the corridors, before or after our gig, with sax and clarinet in my hands, and those dancing girls came rushing past, it was different,' he laughs. 'But we got to the stage where we took no notice. They would stop us and ask about holidays in Europe, and where were the best places to go. Their act was just part and parcel of entertainment at that venue. They were exceptionally good dancers. It wasn't just a gimmick, as they danced so well to the popular rock numbers of the time.'

The Big 8 had their own Irish dancers, and some of those girls had worked previously in Vegas with Brendan, Tom and The Royal Showband. Paddy played Irish jigs and reels on the tin whistle for them during the Irish dancing section of The Big 8's show, which always went down a treat with American audiences. 'Some of the Irish dancers changed from time to time, as some of them got fed up with America and went back home to do something else. We rehearsed their routine inside out with them, and all we had to do was get accustomed to the tunes they would be dancing to,' says Paddy.

At the other side of the building, in the main hall of the casino, some spectacular shows were put on. 'All the girls across the casino, in the main room, had to be at least six foot three, and they often had big head gear on them, making them look eight feet tall. That hall was so vast, and they had a stage that went in and came back out as an ice rink with people skating on it. At the end of one show there, and this is hard to believe, they even had horses charging across the stage. On another occasion, a helicopter would land there as part of the act. That shows you the vastness of the place.

'I remember being there with our showband colleague Larry Cunningham. He was visiting from Ireland, and Tom Dunphy took him to see the show. Back home, Larry was involved in the Ballyjamesduff Follies, a festival of music and comedy held in a small hall in Cavan. When he came out afterwards, I asked Larry what he thought. He smiled, and quipped that he "got a few ideas for the Follies in Ballyjamesduff". I said, "If you bring that show back home, with horses, an ice rink and a helicopter on the stage, it will be some night in Ballyjamesduff!"'

Sometimes when you meet your heroes, it can be exciting, but it can be problematic too. That's what Paddy discovered when he became friends with his boyhood hero, cowboy movie star Roy Rogers. They struck up a friendship after meeting in Vegas. But it evolved into a series of late-night drinking sessions on the strip.

'Roy was in Vegas making one of the modern cowboy movies. Instead of riding on his horse Trigger, he was driving a pickup truck. He came to our show and enjoyed it, particularly Tom Dunphy singing the country songs. We were thrilled to meet him. But even though he was one of the wealthiest men in California, we felt he was a lonely man. While in Vegas making the movie, he was on his own a lot of the time. He would be at the stage door waiting for us to finish every night, hoping to go to the bar with us. Some of the boys started ducking and diving to avoid him. I always seemed to be the victim joining him in the bar. I had told him about how I used to scrape the fourpence together to watch his movies as a child back home. He was a nice guy, but the regular late-night bar sessions became too frequent.

'When the late Kevin Marron of the *Sunday World* newspaper came over on an assignment, Helen and I invited him to our apartment one evening for a meal. The phone rang, and I said to Helen, "If it's Roy Rogers, just tell him I'm not in." Kevin thought this was hilarious; he nearly fell off the seat laughing. Of course, when he went back home, he printed that story in the *Sunday World.*' The story also inspired the title of Tim Ryan's 1975 book on Paddy Cole, *Tell Roy Rogers I'm Not In*.

Kevin died tragically in a plane crash some years later. When Paddy arrived at his funeral Mass in Dundalk, it was so crowded that he couldn't get in. Standing outside, he heard loud laughter coming from the crowd in the church. 'It was when Father Brian D'Arcy told the story, during his homily, about me asking Helen to tell Roy Rogers I wasn't in,' says Paddy.

With Dale Evans and Roy Rogers, Las Vegas, mid-1970s.

The Cole children were young when they lived in Las Vegas. Pearse was four and had started school there before they left. Pat was younger, and Karen was born when they lived there, though Helen went home for her birth. 'A friend of ours, Mick Grant, was a surgeon with his own clinic in Michigan, and he wanted Helen to fly up there to have the baby. But I wanted Karen to be born in Ireland and to be an Irish citizen. Ironically, after all that, Karen is now married and living in Boston, and is an American citizen,' laughs Paddy.

While they lived in Vegas the older children became friendly with the children of Canadian superstar singer-songwriter Paul Anka, as Paddy recalls. 'Andy Anka, Paul's father, lived in the apartment beside us and he was a genuinely nice man. He was also Paul's manager at that time. We would often be relaxing by the pool, chatting to Andy during the day. When Paul's kids were having a birthday party, he would bring our children to the party with Paul's kids. That happened a few times.'

On stage at the Stardust, many of the men attending shows by The Big 8 were huge fans of Twink. 'Twink would sing the popular hit "I've Got a Brand-New Pair of Roller Skates" and, typical of the Americans that were falling for her, they would all bring her roller skates. She ended up with presses full of roller skates. Each one that would bring her a present up to the stage thought they were the only one bringing her roller skates.

'Twink was immensely popular and she had a great way with people everywhere. She got to know a lot of the big stars in Las Vegas and was invited to lots of parties with them. Those stars might be doing two or three weeks there in Caesar's Palace, and some of them would come to see our show at the Stardust. They were all extremely impressed by Twink's

Fishing on the Colorado River, 1972.

talent, as well as some of the girls that did the Irish dancing segment with us. Many of the locals would also invite us to parties in their houses, often on Sunday afternoons or maybe on Tuesday nights when we were off. The people in Vegas were always genuinely nice to us.'

Paddy says that his father's words about never drinking before going on stage kept ringing in his ears. As time went by, he realised how easy it could be to go down the slippery slope to alcoholism. 'We were off every Tuesday night, and there were always parties to go to if you were inclined to do so. We could also go for free to any show on the strip on our night off – Caesar's Palace, the Sands, the Desert Inn or any of the others. All we had to do was go to one of the bosses at the Stardust and say what show we wished to go to. We would immediately get complimentary tickets.

'But on a lot of nights when we weren't playing, Helen and I would just go to the movies. We would hire a babysitter and go for a meal first, and the movies afterwards. We just had to try to establish some semblance of normality, because Vegas could eat you up and spit you out if you let it. Sadly, we saw a lot of people go down the slippery slope there.'

Monday nights were the toughest nights of the week to be an entertainer in Las Vegas. 'There would only be the losers left in Vegas after the weekend, the ones who had lost everything. They might not even have enough money to leave Vegas. They had been fleeced at the gambling tables, and were maybe waiting for someone to send them the fare to go home. Doing three shows on a Monday night was always difficult. We were on the revolving stage, and when we came around to face the crowd, some of them would just be glaring up at us. The looks on their faces seemed to say, "Entertain us!" It was a big challenge for us every Monday night to win over the audience.'

Paddy remembers British entertainer Lonnie Donegan, famous for his skiffle songs and comedy, failing to 'cut the mustard' with the moody Monday night Vegas audiences, or indeed any night that he played there.

'Lonnie talked so fast with his Cockney accent that the Americans couldn't understand what he was saying. He knew he wasn't going down well, and as he said to Tom Dunphy afterwards, he knew he wouldn't be booked back again. So he tried a type of reverse psychology on the audiences. He would come out on stage and say, "Good evening, opposition!" That was his opener. The bosses would say to him afterwards, "That's not particularly good, Lonnie." He would reply that he knew he wouldn't be back anyway. We enjoyed his shows, and thought he was brilliant. But he would say with a laugh, "I'm dying a death here – they don't know what I'm saying or singing." He was philosophical about it.'

Even though Las Vegas is known as Sin City, there are a lot of saints as well as sinners living there, according to Paddy. The Coles went to Mass in Vegas every Saturday evening, and the church they attended would be packed. There would often be some famous faces there. One person they saw there regularly was actor Gianni Russo, who played the part of Carlo Rizzi, the husband of The Godfather's daughter, in that blockbuster film. Paddy says there were 'churches of all sorts' in Vegas.

Due to their popularity in Vegas, when they had free dates available The Big 8 were in demand to play shows from Toronto to Evansville, Indiana. 'One night a man named Bob Greene came up to me after one of our shows in the Stardust, saying he was interested in booking us to play in Evansville. Initially I thought he was a spoofer, as some Americans can be. But as it unfolded, he was very genuine and a very wealthy guy. This man had the contract for constructing all the motorways in that area of Indiana.

Some members of The Big 8 in Evansville, Indiana, 1974: Mickey O'Neill, Jimmy Conway, Dave Coady, Tom Dunphy and Paddy.

'We eventually went out there to play for him, in two magnificent hotels that he owned, with beautiful night clubs in each. One was in Vincennes and the other in Evansville, which were cities not far apart. We played there for a few weeks. He flew us out in his own private jet to the nearest airport, and we were taken the rest of the journey in his private helicopters. He even had a resident big band in the clubs to play support to us. It was something different for us to do gigs like that, and more exciting than the regular ones every night in the one venue in Vegas. It suited us, as there were weeks when we wouldn't work each year while visas and permits were being renewed. At one such time I also organised a trip to Toronto to play in a club there.'

Working under the bright lights of Las Vegas was exciting for Paddy, but he and Helen saw a darker side looming for the family if they stayed there too long. He spoke about stories he had heard about drugs on RTÉ's *A Little Bit Showband* in 2011: 'The drug pushers started handing out sweets outside the school gate in Vegas. There would be drugs in the sweets, and they gave them to kids for nothing first. Then they charged them fifty cents, and next time it was a dollar and so on. It was really for the sake of our children that we decided to get them out of that environment.'

When they discussed the possibility of going back home, Helen revealed that she had been unhappy for much of the time in Vegas. 'We were talking over a cup of tea one day, and I said to Helen that perhaps we should think seriously about not going back to Vegas after our 1974 Irish tour. She was delighted, but I didn't realise until then that she missed Ireland so much. She missed the seasons back home, the daffodils, the green fields, the snow and even the Irish rain. Everything was the same in Vegas all year, every year, but because my job was there she put up with the sameness of the place.

PADDY COLE'S DUBLIN DEBUT

PADDY COLE can feel confident about the future of his band. The crowd for their Dublin debut in the Tara Club loved them. They battle against the Bowyer legend and the power of the Big 8, but that's not going to bother them . . . They opened dramatically with River Deep, Mountain High. Twink and returned Canadian chanter, Pat Morris shared the vocals. That's a belter for a start. They finish with it, too, though inevitably their encore finale was Resurrection Shuffle. Their programme is mainly pop though their country section is adequately handled by their bass man, Mike Dalton, who honours Big Tom by warbling a track of his album, Smoke Along The Track. He's a tall pleasant looking man himself. They're not short of singing power as everyone save organist Michael Keane and trumpeter Ray Moore sing. And Moore harmonises on some as well as taking an instrumental solo on Wonderland By Night. He combines with Paddy Cole on a dixieland jazz medley later, Paddy playing flute. Paddy sings a few, too, amongst them Abbeyshrule. Mickey O'Neill even comes forward for the Did You Ever duet with Twink while Cole covers on drums. Guitarist Jimmy Conway is a big bonus. His amicable disposition is so evident/unlike the switched-on smile of his former Bye-Laws partner, Pat Morris, out front. Jimmy sings a lot, too, which is nice. Black Eyed Boys, Got To Get You Into My Life and Annie's Song were some we recall. And what of their front folk, Twink and Pat Morris? Well neither is sparing in efforts to get across. In fact Morris looks as if he's being crucified during Unchanted Melody, he tries that hard. His Love Me For A Reason came over more naturally. He takes Long Tall Glasses a pace too fast. I liked Twink on You're My World and You're Not Woman Enough (a stirring drama performance here) rather than in those inane numbers in current charts

—Julie Boyd

● Liam Quigley took the pics.

A page from a fan magazine, 1974/75.

'At that time, I had just finished reading a book by a former head of General Motors named Lee Iacocca. His book said that nobody should stay any longer than five years in the same job if they were getting into a rut. He advised people not to stay in the same place unless they wanted to remain there permanently. I said to myself that I certainly didn't want to stay permanently in Vegas – we wanted to eventually make our home in Ireland.

'We were in Ireland during the 1974 tour when we made the decision. We had a car and trunk-loads of stuff left in Vegas, but I just phoned a friend there, Ronnie Scanlon, and told him to give it all to charity if he wished.'

Back home, Paddy had no work planned. But his friend, the late Tony Loughman, one of Ireland's most successful music promoters, heard that he was contemplating not going back to Vegas. Tony phoned him, and that was how the idea for the Paddy Cole Superstars band was born. For the Coles, the Las Vegas odyssey was over.

Chapter 9

Back Home to Blood, Sweat and Tears

The Ireland that Paddy Cole and his family returned to in 1974 was a rapidly changing one, especially economically and educationally. Joining the European Economic Community (EEC) in 1973 was a seismic change for the country. In the 1970s, Ireland started reaping rewards from the seeds of economic progress sown by the Séan Lemass government, and his economist Dr TK Whitaker, in the early to mid-1960s. Social change was happening too in the South, as its young population increased dramatically.

Sadly, in Northern Ireland, the 'Troubles' still raged on. Indeed, 1974, the year the Coles returned, was one of the most tumultuous of all in the North. A power-sharing Northern Ireland Executive collapsed after five months. Deaths and destruction were everywhere, and spreading to the South and to England also. Thirty-three people were killed and over 300 injured in the Dublin and Monaghan bombings by the Ulster Volunteer Force (UVF) in May 1974.

The IRA took their campaign to London in November of that year, bombing the King's Arms in Woolwich. A second ceasefire between the IRA and the British in December was over by April 1975, before the Paddy Cole Superstars had taken to the road. The religious and historical Northern divide seemed a deeper abyss than ever to bridge.

When Paddy returned to Ireland and started his band, he said they planned to play 'everything from country to Blood, Sweat and Tears'. But sadly, in the Ireland of the 1970s, he saw blood, sweat, tears and fatalities too, among his close colleagues, unwittingly drawn into the cauldron of hate. Before that sad summer of 1975, when many commentators say that the showbands died, Paddy also had a less than pleasant parting with The Big 8.

'It was very embarrassing, and it was wrong the way it was done. To this day, I have qualms of conscience about the way it all unfolded. We were in Ennis, rehearsing with The Big 8 for a big gig at the Rose of Tralee International Festival. Our manager, TJ Byrne, came up to me, firstly on his own, saying he had been asked for a quote by a reporter from the *Evening Press*, regarding me leaving the band. I was flabbergasted and extremely upset. To do it all properly, I should have been sitting down with TJ, Tom and Brendan, telling them that I didn't want to go back to Vegas, but was starting my own band. However, the *Evening Press* scooped the story, and it was published that very evening,' says Paddy.

Somebody working with Tony Loughman's Top Rank agency knew that negotiations with Paddy were taking place, and that person innocently told someone else, who leaked it to the media. Paddy hadn't planned to hand in his notice to The Big 8 until he was sure that the band he was putting together was going to become a reality.

Of course, Brendan Bowyer and Tom Dunphy were shocked, upset and annoyed to read in the *Evening Press* that Paddy was leaving. It jettisoned any hopes Paddy had of a smooth transition from one band to another. 'Tom and Brendan came up to me to question me about all of this. As several others were also leaving with me, all I could say was that we were going to give them two or three weeks' notice. I asked them could we discuss it later, after the Tralee gig.

'Anyway, we went on to Tralee to set up the equipment for the show. But that night, Tom Dunphy said they had cancelled all the dates for the next few weeks, and they didn't want our two or three weeks' notice. I had the unenviable task of going to Tom and saying that while I wasn't expecting any pay, the other boys who were leaving with me needed a few weeks' holiday pay.

'There was a bit of a dispute about that, but then, out of the blue, Bill Fuller arrived to mediate. He asked me, was my mind completely made up? I replied that it was, and that it was for family reasons and not due to any falling out with Tom or Brendan. Bill was very fair with me about it, and said he would not put any pressure on me to stay. But I said to Bill that he needed to talk sense to Tom Dunphy, as I didn't want to be going down a legal road to get it sorted out. I again said that the other boys had to get their pay for two weeks, and in fairness to Tom and Brendan, they agreed. It was a sad way to have to end it all.

'Twink eventually joined the new band, but it took some convincing to get her to join. She had left The Big 8 before me. Twink was a big star, and to be honest, we weren't including her enough in our programme with The Big 8. Following the death, in an accident, of a cousin in Ireland who she was awfully close to, she had become more unsettled in America and decided to go back home. Her plans included doing more theatre work, which she had also done earlier in her career. She was also working at an equestrian centre in Dublin, as she was big into training horses and working with them.

'I went to see her, and asked if she would come back into a Paddy Cole band that Tony Loughman was interested in putting on the road. She said she would think about it. Tony Loughman and others spoke to her about it, and when it was clear that some of the other lads in The Big 8 were staying at home, that convinced her to do it. So we had the nucleus of a band before the story broke prematurely in the press.'

When The Paddy Cole Superstars played their first date, both Tom Dunphy and Brendan Bowyer graciously came along. 'It was in the Tara Club in Dublin, and it was packed. As I was walking up to the bandstand, I saw Tom sitting with a crowd of people. I still have terrible regrets that I didn't go over and chat with him, but I didn't. I wasn't sure what sort of a reception I would have got if I did. But later, after Tom was killed in a car crash, it played on my mind that I should have gone over and talked to him that night. Tom was a gentleman, as was Brendan, and there was no acrimony between us.'

The only three originals now left in The Big 8 were Brendan, Tom and Dave Coady. They went on to replace Paddy, and all the others, with high-quality musicians. But Brendan said later during a radio interview that the band was never the same after Paddy left.

The Paddy Cole Superstars didn't take to the road for a month after the split, as Paddy explains: 'We were rehearsing and getting the new band ready for the launch, and firming up on the final line-up. Ray Moore came in from The Plattermen, playing trumpet and keyboards. Later, when some of the lads went back to The Big 8, there was no animosity and we replaced them with other talented musicians. Pat Morris, who came home from Canada, was the first lead singer to record a debut disc with the band, titled "Mother Was Her Name". Another singer who also came back from Canada to join the Paddy Cole band for a time was Derrick Mehaffey.'

The Paddy Cole Superstars were a massive attraction in the North of Ireland, pulling huge crowds everywhere they played, their fans being from all religions and none. The Paddy Cole Superstars released an album on the Harmac record label, and Paddy got a Silver Disc for sales of the record. 'There is a photo in my collection where I am jokingly threating to smash the Silver Disc over Phil Coulter's head, at the presentation. Phil was recording with the same label at that time,' recalls Paddy with a laugh.

While The Paddy Cole Superstars did some tours abroad, they never played in Las Vegas, though they could have if they had wished to. 'Bill Fuller approached me to see if I would take the band to Vegas. He had a hotel lined up for us to play in. But that would only have defeated the whole reason for me leaving The Big 8, which was so that our family could move home to Ireland.'

Paddy was approached again and asked to re-join The Big 8 after tragedy struck the band, when Tom Dunphy died in a horrific road crash in Leitrim on 29 July 1975. Paddy recalls that fateful evening: 'The Big 8 were playing

Above: The Paddy Cole Band:
Back: Mickey O'Neill, Paddy, Twink, Jimmy Conway, Mike Dalton;
Front: Michael Keane, Pat Morris, Ray Moore.
Below: Another line-up of The Paddy Cole Band:
Tony Hughes, Ray Moore, Paddy, Twink, Pat Sharkey, Colm Hughes, Jimmy Smyth.

Above: The Paddy Cole Band:
Frankie Murray, Paddy, Bram McCarthy, Stan Byrne, Mike Dalton,
Mickey O'Neill;
Front: Tony O'Leary.
Below: Paddy brandishing a silver disc at Phil Coulter.

at the Mary From Dungloe Festival in Donegal, and that's where Tom was heading for. At one stage, maybe near Monasterevin, we met a car going around a corner and some the boys in the band said that Tom Dunphy was the driver. I said if I'd known that, I would have flashed the lights at him.

'We were going to Ballybunion in Kerry, where we were playing that night. After we had a meal, I went back into the ballroom and somebody said that Twink was extremely upset and crying. So, when I got to where Twink was I discovered that a phone call had come to the hotel for me, and Twink had said that she would take a message. The message was that Tom Dunphy had been killed in a car crash. It was a terrible night to have to go on and play. Subsequently I went down to Tramore in Waterford for Tom's funeral. As you can imagine, there was a huge outpouring of grief for Tom.'

Further tragedy was to hit the Irish music world just two nights later, when the horrific ambush known as the Miami Showband Massacre happened in County Down. Paddy got the news as he was travelling from the south to Dublin. The air was balmy, with a tang of the River Liffey in it, on that slightly foggy summer's morning. Dublin was almost devoid of traffic as a tired Paddy Cole drove along a near-deserted O'Connell Street at 5am. He was still coming to terms with the sad passing of Tom when his thoughts, in the stillness of that summer's morning in Dublin, were shattered.

'I was returning to Dublin from a gig down the country in the early hours. Often when doing so, I would buy a newspaper from a seller on O'Connell Bridge. I would roll down the window and simply say "Indo". He would usually laughingly reply, "Indeed O." But that morning, his face was more serious. He told me that reporter Tony Wilson of the *Irish Independent* had been called in to work overnight. The newspaper seller was in the *Independent* office, collecting his papers, when he heard that Tony was called in because something, maybe a crash, had happened involving a showband. The only other details he heard was that there may have been fatalities and that it was "somewhere up north".

'When I got home, I phoned the newsroom of the *Irish Independent*, and Tony Wilson answered the call. He only had sketchy information at that stage – that it was The Miami, and that there were several deaths. He thought it might have been a crash; he didn't know then that they had been shot during an ambush.

'There was no going to bed for me after that. Slowly, the horrible news filtered through that they had been shot and several of them were dead. It was such an awful week. Those of us in the music business spent days attending the funerals of our friends and colleagues. I still keep in touch with Stephen Travers of The Miami, who was severely injured in the shooting and is still fighting the good fight to try to get justice. He believes that without a shadow of doubt, there was collusion between the loyalist terrorists involved in the ambush and the British Army. There has been a long-held view that [Captain] Nairac was there, running the whole operation from the background. It is believed that when the bomb the terrorists were planting in The Miami's bandwagon blew up, killing two of them, there was panic, and they started shooting the band members.

'Days later, still in a daze, I remember going out to Bray, to Fran O'Toole's funeral. Never, ever, will I forget the grief of his poor father, trying to grab the coffin. It was horrendous.'

The alleged involvement of British Army intelligence officer, Captain Robert Nairac, is said to have been confirmed recently in 'heavily redacted British Ministry of Defence papers released to the lawyer for the family of one of the victims'. (Ciaran Tierney, Irish Central website, 30 January 2020). Two years after the Miami Massacre, Nairac is alleged to have been abducted and shot by the IRA. His body has never been found.

Many showbands would not play in Northern Ireland after that atrocity, and for a time The Paddy Cole Superstars were among those who feared to do so. 'While we always had huge crowds everywhere in the North, we were never that popular in the South. When we had an exceedingly small crowd one night at a dance in the Longford Arms hotel, some months after the massacre, the writing was really on the wall for us. I called a band meeting and said that, while I was not pressuring anyone, we had to make up our minds whether we would play in the North again. We could either fold up the band, and I would tell this to Tony Loughman, or else go back to playing in the North.

'They all decided we should keep the band going, and go back up North. We were the first showband to do so, and both communities welcomed us with open arms. The ballrooms were packed to capacity everywhere. It opened up the entertainment scene again in the North when we went back to play there. Other bands started to come up again from the South, and bands in the North itself, who hadn't been playing due to fear, started playing once more. The whole scene opened again, and it was wonderful to see that happen. In Belfast, we played in venues where the audiences were predominantly Protestant. We also played in places there where the audiences were predominantly Catholic, and we played to mixed audiences at many other venues. The conflict was never an issue with the dancers, who simply loved music. It never affected us regarding where we played. We were there to entertain people, irrespective of religion, and we did our best to entertain everyone.'

If he had wished to, Paddy could have avoided the issue of going back to playing in the North – by accepting another offer from The Big 8 to re-join them in Las Vegas. 'Following the tragic death of Tom Dunphy, promoter Frank McLoone phoned me to ask if I would meet some people in the Gresham hotel in Dublin. He said there were a few people who wanted to talk to me, but there was no pressure being exerted on me if I didn't want to meet them. I was in Monaghan, but as Frank was a gentleman, who I could trust, there was no issue with me driving to Dublin to meet him. When I arrived at the meeting, there were Brendan Bowyer, TJ Byrne and Jimmy Cooke, who was an accountant for The Big 8. Sadly, all three have since passed away.

'Frank did the introductions and said that he was only there as the convenor of the meeting. They asked if I would fold up The Paddy Cole Superstars and go back into The Big 8 as bandleader. I said no, because Tony Loughman had put a lot of money into forming The Paddy Cole Superstars. Amplification equipment, instruments, a tour bus and everything else needed by a band had been purchased. Tony also had a full diary of dates for us across Northern Ireland, and I couldn't let him down. I had had enough of Vegas anyway from the years that I was there, and while I appreciated their approach, I told them I wasn't interested.

'Then Frank McLoone interjected, saying he was surprised I had made up my mind before I had even heard what the offer was. This was the reason that Jimmy Cooke, the accountant, was at the meeting. My exact words in response were, "Please do not even reveal the offer to me." That was because I knew there might be cold Irish nights when I would be putting up band equipment in cold ballrooms and longing for Las Vegas in the heat. So they never told me what their offer was. Long afterwards, Frank told me that they had a good offer worked out for me, including even a percentage of the takings. The Dublin meeting ended quickly and very amicably. I also heard that Bill Fuller was in the background regarding that offer. If I had accepted, he would have put things in motion in Vegas. But I wasn't for moving.'

Many other great musicians played in The Big 8 after that, including Pat Chesters, who had been in The Plattermen; Paddy Reynolds, who was formerly with The Casino Showband; and singer and saxophonist DJ Curtin from The Kerry Blues band. 'Shortly after Tom Dunphy's death, they also got country singer Frankie Carroll, who had been lead vocalist with a band called The Ranchers. I was involved in financing The Ranchers, but Jim Hand's office, who were managing them, were more interested in pop bands. They didn't get a fair crack of the whip regarding promotion. Frankie Carroll should have been a country superstar, with the voice that he had. He was fantastic,' says Paddy.

Three of the original Big 8 – Jimmy Conway, Michael Keane and Mickey O'Neill – eventually left Paddy's band and re-joined The Big 8. They went back to Las Vegas, while The Paddy Cole Superstars went back to playing in the North of Ireland. 'The North remained big for us, as Tony Loughman had geared most of the publicity towards Northern venues and Northern media. I remember playing in Cookstown, County Tyrone, for Big Brendan Mulgrew, and the dancers would be outside queuing up three deep along the street waiting for the band. The story was the same all over the North.'

Paddy soon had another business venture going on in Castleblayney in tandem with the music. 'We were incredibly happy living in Dublin, with the kids going to school there and having their own group of friends. But with The Superstars doing so much work in the North, I was travelling to and from Castleblayney all the time. Helen and I decided to relocate

Tony Loughman, promoter extraordinaire.

back to County Monaghan. As Tony Loughman had several vacant houses outside the town, we were initially staying in one of those, in Annalitten. The kids went to a little country school there, which was great, and I was delighted about that. Then we started building a house of our own.

'Around this time, a friend of mine was selling his bar and restaurant in Castleblayney, and I thought it would be a good idea to have a business as well as the band. I was putting myself into a lot of debt with bank borrowings, but we bought the premises anyway. Suddenly, I was in the bar business, which was completely new to me. Between the house building and the band, the pub plus the borrowings, I don't know how we survived,' laughs Paddy.

The pub was formerly called Mac Moore's, but was renamed 'Paddy Cole's Place'. It had a restaurant upstairs, which Helen took control of. As stated in Tim Ryan's *Tell Roy Rogers I'm Not In*, 'Helen Cole, a student of Cathal Brugha St, used her skills to introduce some fresh food ideas to the people of Co. Monaghan and surrounding areas.'

As time went by, Paddy had to deal with musicians leaving to be replaced by others. But he says they were lucky, because the new ones were as good as, or in some instances better than, those they replaced. 'Young Jimmy Smyth was a brilliant guitarist, as was Big Ronnie O'Flynn who was on bass. Ray Moore on trumpet did a lot of the arrangements with me. Twink was out front on vocals, and it was a great band,' says Paddy.

Even if they were lucky with replacement musicians, Paddy would have preferred to have a stable line-up for as long as possible. 'I really hated change, but Tony Loughman was a rock when it came to that. When the boys told me that they wanted to go back to Vegas, after a gig in Dundalk one night, I was shocked. I met Tony Loughman first thing the next morning, when Mike "Buddy" Dalton from Kerry on bass, Twink and I were the only ones left in the band. But Tony was the coolest person ever about changing personnel in a band. I said, "What are we going to do about all those leaving?" He responded, cool as could be, saying, "We will just replace them," and I nearly fainted. But he was right. He replaced them with Colm and Tony Hughes, who were great guys, and subsequently Colm came out front on vocals. Then Butch McNeill came in on drums and Gerry Black, formerly of The Seasons, joined us on vocals and keyboards. Micky McCarthy, another great guitarist, came in later when Jimmy Smyth left. Micky did all the tours with Johnny Logan after Johnny won the Eurovision.'

More dark clouds were looming on the horizon for The Paddy Cole Superstars, as Twink decided that she was leaving to go into cabaret in Dublin. Paddy was also dealing with excruciating back pain, and was off the stage for a time and in hospital. When he returned, he was in for a bigger shock, as he was sacked from the band! 'I was told I was too old to be in such a youthful band – but, bloody hell, I was only about forty at the time. So they were going to start hitting a younger and different audience. All I could say was fair play to them, and with Colm Hughes out front, they had the right idea. Tony Loughman said that he would like me to have a new role as promotions manager for the band.'

Paddy was less than enamoured with this sideways promotion, judging by his reaction on an RTÉ 1 TV programme at that time. He was a guest on Donncha Ó Dúlaing's *Highways and Byways* programme. There was surprise, but almost a monotone flatness and lack of enthusiasm, in Paddy's answer to Donncha's question, 'Why are the Paddy Cole Superstars minus you now?' 'Well,' replied Paddy, 'I have been off the stage now, Donncha, for about four or five months. I am doing promotional work for the band instead. An old fellow like me doesn't fit into that scene now. But as you can see, they are the best band you've had on your programme yet. However, there is no place for someone of my age in that young line-up.' But he didn't sound convincing, even when Donncha said that what he liked about Paddy was his modesty.

Now, forty years later, Paddy can laugh about it all. 'I knew that this was a made-up sort of a job title. It was work for someone in an office, sending out posters to ballrooms and hotels. I did it for a little while, but without any great enthusiasm. I got sick of it very quickly and said that I would rather be playing music, irrespective of what group I would be in.'

Soon Twink was to ask Paddy to play at some of her shows in Dublin, and that is what got him started on the cabaret scene. 'Twink probably bushwhacked me into doing cabaret. She invited Helen and I to a show she was doing in Clontarf Castle, and we were really impressed. When the show was over, Anne D'Arcy, the manageress of the venue, asked if I would be a special guest on the next show that Twink was doing there, a few weeks later. I did so, and then Twink said that the Braemor Rooms, another big Dublin cabaret venue, wanted me to do the same. Suddenly I was doing the cabaret scene, and I liked it. The musicians in the bands were good, and it was enjoyable doing my guest spot. I might have bookings for two or three weeks at a time at each venue in Dublin, while I was still running the bar in Castleblayney.'

The band that Paddy had got 'the sack' from was renamed The Super-stars, with Colm Hughes out front as their lead singer. 'All in all, I would say the band lasted roughly from 1975 to approximately 1981 or '82. But I had gone from the band when Colm took over and it was renamed The Superstars.'

In recent years, there was a reunion of the band, with Paddy back as a member, in his hometown of Castleblayney. A family called Watters have a bar and cabaret venue in the town, and in 2019, they held a 'Welcome Back to Castleblayney' night at their venue for Paddy Cole. 'Colm Hughes put The Superstars back together for the gig, and we had a fantastic night. The crowds were out the door it was so packed. I went down there early to practise and to work out what sort of programme we were going to do. We got together for some coffee first, but as we stayed talking for two hours or more about old times, there was no rehearsal. We just went up on the stage and straight into playing, and it went great.

'Plans were put in place for a similar get-together in July 2020. Of course, Covid-19 scuttled that, but we will be back playing there again sometime, please God.'

Chapter 10

Shots Inside the Pub and Outside!

Paddy grew accustomed to having to bar people from his bar as well as serving shots. But some of his covert customers ended up firing shots outside in the street when uncovered, after leaving, to be undercover agents. It was all part of a publican's life in a bar in a border town during the 'Troubles' in Northern Ireland. In those years, Paddy had all sorts of customers, especially when the place was packed for the Monday night music sessions there.

'You wouldn't want to bar the wrong person, but I made a rule that if anyone was out of order, or caused a row in the pub, they were barred for life. That word spread extremely fast. A man from Armagh came back to me about a year after he had been barred and told me he had given up the drink. I felt sorry for him, but I couldn't go back on my word and serve him, even though he only wanted a soft drink. On the Monday nights, we had people from all walks of life at the music sessions. We had off-duty Gardaí, off-duty Army men, off-duty customs officials, IRA members, INLA members, smugglers. It was like a powder keg on Monday nights. But nobody ever made a wrong move,' says Paddy.

While his customers came from both side of the border, he says if any loyalists were among them, they kept their identities quiet. Some undercover British Army agents were in the bar one night, with the intention of accosting some republicans who they thought might be drinking there. But the undercover agents were uncovered later that night 'down the street', and shots were fired when they were cornered.

'We only found out about those British Army undercover agents afterwards. They were trying to snatch a few IRA fellows who were staying in Castleblayney. The story of shots being fired on the street made the *Times* in London. The agents were obviously in plain clothes, and had been drinking in our pub, and then they went down the street to where there was a dance. One of them took a girl out to dance, and he happened to say to her, "I don't see such-and-such a fellow here tonight." She knew that the fellow *was* there.

'Realising that the guy she was dancing with was fishing for information, she warned the other fellow that he was being watched. The other guys confronted the undercover agents and they were bashed out onto the street. They felt they were cornered at one stage, and one of them pulled out a revolver and fired a few shots. People here were annoyed that the Gardaí took them by squad car to the barracks, before escorting them across the border and letting them go.

Micky McCarthy on bass, Jimmy Smyth on vocal and guitar, Maurice Lynch on trumpet, 25 January 1982, Paddy Cole's pub, Castleblayney.

'You never knew who was in the pub on a busy night. But that was the way it was back then; those were the times that were in it.'

While most of the pub bombings and shootings were in the North, it must have been a terrifying time for any publican on either side of the Irish border. The worst pub bombing of all was in Belfast, a few years before Paddy came back to Ireland. That was in McGurk's Pub in Belfast, in December 1971. On that terrible night, fifteen Catholics, including two children, died, and seventeen others were injured. Paramilitary terrorist group the Ulster Volunteer Force (UVF) were responsible for the bombing, which caused the pub to collapse.

Equally horrific were the IRA bombings of pubs in Birmingham and Woolwich in the UK. Those atrocities took place in 1974, the year the Coles returned to Ireland, and when The Paddy Cole Superstars started playing. The Monaghan and Dublin bombings by loyalist terrorists were also that year, followed by the bombings of two pubs in Guildford by the IRA and then the Miami Massacre by loyalists in 1975. Also in 1975, a pub in Dundalk was bombed by loyalists, killing two civilians. In March 1976, a car bomb by loyalists in Castleblayney, where the Coles were to buy their pub three years later, killed one and injured seventeen.

Other horrific attacks on pubs during the 'Troubles' included the killing of eleven British soldiers and six civilians by the Irish National Liberation Army (INLA) at the Droppin' Well pub and disco at Ballykelly, County Derry, in December 1982. A further thirty on the premises were injured. Loyalists targeted the Rising Sun bar in Greysteel, County Derry, killing eight and wounding nineteen; and O'Toole's Bar in Loughinisland, County Down, killing six customers and wounding five others. Those two incidents were in the early 1990s, after Paddy had left the pub business.

However, those are only some of the bombings, shootings and attacks on bars during the Northern 'Troubles'. It must have been a worrying time.

As well as having terrorists, paramilitaries, undercover agents and rowdy customers to deal with, there was a little bit of small-town jealousy too. But Paddy says it was miniscule, and it was 'just competition' in business. 'There were one or two who resented us doing good business. But when we had the music on a Monday night, and our place would be packed, one publican near us often said, "I love the Monday nights, because we are packed as well." A lot of pubs were getting the overflow from our place. Even if there were some people who resented it, there weren't that many really, and it never affected us badly. I took it in my stride and said it was part of business competition. Maybe if I were in their shoes, I would feel the same way.'

The Monday nights, with the music sessions in full swing, were the best nights for business for Paddy. 'Many local musicians joined in. They included Gerry Muldoon, my brother-in-law Ronnie Duffy from The Mainliners, his son Mark, my old bandleader Maurice Lynch, Jimmy Smyth, Gabriel McQuillian, Micky McCarthy and many more. It was like a who's who of great musicians playing together. The people really appreciated it and enjoyed those sessions.'

The entertainers clearly enjoyed themselves too. Many, including famous folk stars The Fureys, The Sands Family, Mark Alfred (now MD with Riverdance), Colm Hughes and Ronnie O'Flynn, have said so to Paddy since. 'Some of them would have a drink after the music sessions, and those who didn't drink usually had a good strong mug of Monaghan tay [tea],' laughs Paddy.

In 1983 and '84 came the two reunions of The Capitol Showband, which took Paddy on tour nationwide again. That obviously put extra pressure

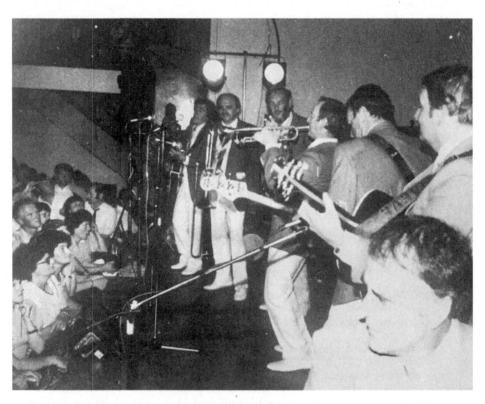

The Capitol Showband on stage during their 1984 reunion tour, Salthill, Galway.

Paddy playing at an open-air fundraiser for Trócaire, 1990s.

Above: Marie and Seamus Heaney, Helen and Paddy, 2013.
Below: The Paddy Cole Band with Maureen O'Hara at Foynes. Her husband was the first transatlantic pilot to land in Foynes: Ronnie Duffy, Pat McCarthy, Paddy, Maureen O'Hara, Reg Lloyd, Gordon Reynolds.

Above: The Paddy Cole Band, pre-gig, c.2010: Michael Inight, Paddy, Ronnie Duffy, Reg Lloyd, Pat McCarthy.
Below: On tour in the Middle East, early 2000s, with Jimmy Hogan on banjo.

Above: Paddy's mother's birthday celebration:
back: Lucia, Carmel, Paddy, Mai and Betty;
front: Jacinta, mother Mary 'Cissie' and Sadie.
Below: Celebrating the wedding of Twink and David Agnew.

Above: A Cole family portrait, celebrating Paddy and Helen's fiftieth wedding anniversary, 2015: top: Sadie, Pat, Ger, Nicky, Pearse, Greg; middle: Ruby, Ava, Paddy, Helen, Edel, Karen and baby Scarlet; front: Keelin, Dillon, Patrick and Jamie Kate.

Below: Pat graduating from TCD. From left: Karen, Paddy, Pat, Helen and Pearse.

Top left: With Goldie Hawn, at the *Late Late Show*.
Above left: Paddy, Terry Sloane and Noel V Ginnity at the unveiling of the mural, 2019.
Above right: With Roly Daniels, showband reunion tour, c.2016.
Below: Backstage at the National Concert Hall at a concert to honour Professor Peter O'Brien. From left: Stride O'Brien, Reg Lloyd, Aonghus Fanning, Pat McCarthy, Paddy, Ronan Kennedy, Stephen McDonald, Ronnie Drew, John Curran, Jimmy Smyth, Mike Hanrahan.

Above: On set at the *Craic'n'Cole* television show, with Marco Petrassi and Sonny Knowles.
Below: A get-together after the Irish Open in Lahinch: Eugene Gilligan, Paddy, Conor O'Brien, Dennis Creedon, Donal Curtin and Des Hanrahan.

Paddy, Helen and family at the unveiling of the mural in Castleblayney, 2019.

PADDY COLE
JAZZ MUSICIAN

Photo: Jimmy Walsh

on his wife Helen and their now teenage family to run the pub. Or did it? 'Well of course it did, but while Helen looked after the restaurant upstairs, my sister Carmel, Ronnie Duffy's wife, worked the bar for us, and she was great at that. A strange aspect about it is that if there were voices raised, or a row brewing, Carmel would go out from behind the bar and tell them to behave. A woman going out and doing that worked with those guys, but if I were there and walked out, I'd probably get a box in the mouth.'

While he was travelling all over Ireland, Paddy was lucky to have his great friend the late Micky (Prandy) Duffy, a former Ulster champion boxer, with him. At other times, the tour promoter, also his friend, Tony Loughman would travel with Paddy to the gigs.

Some highlights from the second year of the reunion tour will be etched in Paddy's mind forever. 'We did a televised show from the Cork Opera House, and Eamonn Campbell (also with The Dubliners) arranged for a string section and a brass section. We did the *Late Late Show* with Gay Byrne during that tour, and those were amazing highlights. Also, the venues were packed everywhere. Not alone did our fans from times past come out, but many brought their teenage kids as well.'

Paddy says that those tours by The Capitol prompted similar reunion tours by other showbands. Several bands who had been off the road for years phoned The Capitol members, asking about how they organised it. Then somebody had the idea of taking a few lead singers and prominent musicians from several bands and putting them on tour with a backing band.

These showband-style tours were remarkably successful, and still are for Ronan Collins of RTÉ, Tommy Swarbrigg, David Hull from Belfast and many more. Paddy worked very closely on tours with Ronan Collins, who

Capitol Showband reunion tour:
Front: Johnny Kelly, Prandy Duffy, Des Kelly;
Back: Paddy, Don Long, Eamon Monahan, Jimmy Hogan, Paul Sweeney, Butch Moore.

had plenty of experience of the showband scene as a former drummer with Dickie Rock's band. 'Ronan and I started off working at cabaret events in Clontarf Castle and the Breamor Rooms. We also did trips abroad with Sean Skehan Golf Tours, performing – and golfing – in Spain, Portugal and the USA. He also put together a successful series of compilation CDs from the showband era, released on Dolphin Discs. Ronan and I also worked on most of showband revival tours promoted by Tommy Swarbrigg.'

The Capitol unlocked the secret of running such tours, and were an education for younger bands too on how they should play. As showbusiness priest Father Brian D'Arcy wrote in 1984 in 'Butch Moore and The Capitol Showband – A Souvenir Programme', 'I firmly believe that before any young band goes on the road, they should be locked in a room for a month with The Capitol, so they can learn what showbusiness, and entertaining, are about.'

In 1984, Paddy was also playing country music at the Rose of Tralee Festival. Two tracks of his appear on a compilation album alongside his friends Susan McCann, Philomena Begley and others. He performed those same two tracks on the RTÉ TV show 'Keep it Country From the Rose of Tralee Festival', presented by Paschal Mooney. The tracks were the Cajun number 'Sally Joe' by Louisiana's Doug Kershaw and 'The Little Country Boy'. The latter song was recently recorded in a similar style by young Irish country singer Gerry Guthrie.

Paddy did both numbers in a jazzier country style that was unmistakeably his own. 'I changed the musical arrangement of the songs around a bit, and put soprano sax or alto sax solos on them. We did a lot of Waylon Jennings stuff in my own band later, and Ronnie Duffy sang a lot of those songs. It wasn't that I disliked country music, as I

Above: At Butch Moore's funeral: Eamon Monahan, Des Kelly, Butch's wife Maeve Mulvaney, Jimmy Hogan, Paddy, Paul Sweeney.
Below: Footballer Kenny Dalglish, Paddy, golfer Ian Woosnam and Chris de Burgh, at a 'Links Society' charity golf event, late 1980s.

am delighted to say that I have very eclectic tastes in music. My taste ranges from Irish traditional music – I love listening to traditional players when I'm in County Clare – to good country music, while I also often listen to classical music, as well as jazz of course.

'When I was living in Castleblayney, I did a lot of session work in Tony Loughman's recording studio, including recordings by Big Tom. He liked the baritone sax, as did Tony Loughman. When Big Tom recorded his popular song "Run to the Door", I played the baritone sax on that session.'

The Capitol Showband reunion tours also reinvigorated Paddy's desire to be back playing, and were massively successful in 1983 and '84, but there was no third tour, for a variety of reasons. Paddy got a huge shock when he heard that Bram McCarthy had passed away, after a heart operation in hospital. He died at a young age in 1987. That same year, the drummer Johnny Kelly, and singer of the number one hit 'The Black Velvet Band', also passed away. He was laid to rest in his native Galway. Butch Moore died in the USA in 2001. Then in 2007, Don Long passed away. Joe Dolan from Galway, a guitarist with the original band before Paddy joined, died in 2008. Jimmy Hogan died in 2016.

Band leader and founder member Des Kelly, who was a well-known voice on Galway Bay FM radio for many years, passed away after a long illness in 2017. Des had launched the careers of many others through his involvement with The Capitol, the Ruby Records label and an artist management agency. Along with Eamon Monahan, Des had hired Paddy Cole for The Capitol. He also helped kickstart the careers of many other singers and musicians, including Christy Moore and Planxty, Phil Coulter, Margo O'Donnell, Mick Hanly, The Smokey Mountain Ramblers and Dermot Henry. In a tribute posted online shortly after his death, Andy Irvine of

Planxty described Des as 'one of the nicest men on the planet, who had managed both Sweeney's Men and Planxty'.

All the members of The Capitol who have since moved on to the great ballroom in the sky were full of zest and enthusiasm especially during their iconic 1984 reunion tour. Those reunion shows with The Capitol are among the most fondly remembered moments of Paddy's career in show business. The tours rekindled a desire in him to leave the bar business and go back to playing music. But the main catalyst for Paddy to pack in the pub business was his family. They left him in no doubt as to why he should leave the pub trade:

'We were relaxing in the sitting room of the house when I asked the two boys which of them would take over the bar when I retired. They both nearly broke their sides laughing at me. They had seen what the work in the bar was like as they helped on busy nights, collecting glasses, often there till the early hours. They had no interest in it, and we respected their views and decided to sell the bar.'

It seems that even before that family meeting, Paddy might have felt that the bar business wasn't a job for life for him either, judging by a comment to journalist Patsy McArdle in the *Sunday Press* in March 1986: 'It's fifteen hours, a day and a night job, but playing music for two hours would pay as much.'

Looking back on those times now though, he has many good memories of his time as a publican. 'I'd have to say that I made a lot of good friends through the bar. Particularly people from the south Armagh direction, who were great customers. Some of them I meet from time to time up to this day. A lot of those people were there the night we did the "Paddy Cole Welcome Home" gig in Watters' of Castleblayney in 2019. While we had

Right: In Tanzania, learning the local dance moves from the Masai Chief. Below: On a undraising walk for the Irish Heart Foundation, South Africa: Martin McArdle, Paddy O'Brien, Paddy, Professor Vincent McBrierty, Helen.

great times, I never figured that I would finish up in the bar for all my life. I felt that at some stage I would be moving back out of the bar business to play music again.'

Moving back to live and work in Dublin was no big issue for Paddy at that point, as his sons Pearse and Patrick were in Trinity College in Dublin, while Karen was away at boarding school. 'As there was only Helen and I that had to make the move, we were both happy to do so. The cabaret shows that I was doing, and most of the corporate work, was in Dublin. While we had put a lot into our house in Castleblayney, with nice gardens and a bit of an orchard, we simply had to move on. The logistics of travelling to and from Dublin was not really practical at that stage, particularly when all our family were away.'

Paddy and Helen settled into living in Dublin again easily, and he says it was a good omen that they bought their home in Ballsbridge, where they still live. 'We looked at several houses, but my buddy from Monaghan, Mick Sherry, who lives close to here, was instrumental in us settling in Ballsbridge. He recommended it to us, and by coincidence, the lady who owned it before us was a Rita Cole.

'There were other coincidences too, which I felt were good omens. When I met the man who was said to be selling it, at a football game in Croke Park, he confirmed that it was on the market. I told him I would meet him the next day at the house. I was on my way to play at a jazz festival weekend in Adare when I went to inspect the house. Walking up the steps to look at it, I noticed that the name plaque over the door had the word "Adare", and that put me thinking too. We did the deal, and are incredibly happy here, as it is so close to central Dublin. Our son Pat and his wife Ger and the four grandchildren live within walking distance of us, which is great,' he adds.

Above: At the Paddy Cole Golf Classic, with (left) Evan Henry (RIP) and (right) Michael Sherry. Below: Helen and her brother John Hehir at Pat Cole's wedding, c.2002.

Paddy and Helen's grandchildren are musical, but none of their own children followed their father into the music business. 'Our eldest son Pearse had no interest in the music; he was always an academic. Pat was a good musician, especially playing the saxophone. When he went to Dublin to study at Trinity, he used to also go a few days a week to the School of Music, and was doing well with his playing.

'Then he went to Germany for a year as an exchange student, and at one stage Helen said to me that Pat was going to bring back an alto sax when coming home on holiday. I replied to her that I knew the old music bug would bite him. But Helen responded that I was going to be disillusioned, because he only wanted to make some money busking. He discovered that buskers at train stations could make a lot of money, and that was what he was going to do during the summer holidays. He, very cutely, said that a busker only needed to know one tune when playing at a train station. Because everybody there is transient, by the time you have finished playing one tune they have gone!

'Our grandchildren, both in America and here at home, are all musical. Sadie Cole is in an orchestra, playing viola, and Ruby Cole is also in an orchestra, playing flute. It was a great pleasure for me to go to the National Concert Hall and see Sadie play, and then to go to concerts and recitals and see Ruby play.'

Paddy's popular regular gig at the Harcourt Hotel, for almost a decade, was a mainstay of his music career in the capital. But enjoyable though it was, there was a darker side to it, which could have led him unwittingly down a slippery slope towards self-destruction. 'I was asked by my friend Brian McGill, who is still a great pal of mine today, if I would do that regular gig on Sunday nights. At the time, he had a three- or four-piece jazz band playing there. But while they were great players, their programme wasn't commercial. I went to see the show, and sadly there was only a small crowd there.

'Brian asked me to try it for a few months. I agreed to do so for three months, to give it my best shot, and build up a following. With the publicity campaign he was putting in place, I was willing to give it a try, and if it didn't work out I would just move out. It became so successful that it lasted for almost ten years,' says Paddy.

Among those in the band for a while was his former musical partner the late Jimmy Hogan. Jimmy played banjo; Jack Bayle was on trombone; Neilus McKenna was on trumpet; Johnny Christopher was on drums and vocals; and Reggie Lloyd was on bass; while Michael Inight, who has since passed on, Lord rest him, was on piano. It was a good Dixieland jazz band, and a lot of other great musicians would sometimes come up and play some tunes with us.

'The late Arty McGlynn was one of those. Arty was a wonderful guitarist, and an exceptional steel guitarist with The Plattermen and later Brian Coll's band The Buckaroos. I knew him since his early days playing back in Omagh, and of course Ray Moore, his colleague from The Plattermen, had also been on trumpet with me in The Paddy Cole Band. We had some amazing sessions in the Harcourt Hotel.'

At that time, Paddy was also 'doing the rounds' of the jazz festivals that were springing up in cities and towns around the country. The most notable of those was the hugely popular Cork Jazz Festival. 'When the Cork one became so successful, a lot of other towns then thought that all they had to do was mention the word "jazz" and they would also have a big festival. Some of them did very well, but others just ended up being music weekends with different music on different nights.'

Above: At the Cork Jazz Festival
with the Billy Crosbie Band:
Piano: Billy Crosbie; trumpet:
Marco Petrassi; clarinet: Paddy;
saxophones: Mick Lynch, Sonny
Knowles and Frank Ireland.
Left: With Joe Mac, drummer
with The Dixies.

While Cork became the premier jazz festival in the South, and Paddy played it for many years, he hasn't performed there in recent times. 'It is still a great festival, but is gone more modern now, with some pop bands on stage there as well. Even when I hadn't my own band, I still went to Cork, and I played at a few festivals there with Billy Crosbie of the famous Cork publishing family. Billy is a great ragtime piano player, and he had a fine band, with my old friend Marco Petrassi in the line-up and Pat McCarthy on trombone and vocals. He had been a member of The Paddy Cole Band years earlier. That band continued doing the venues I used to play in around Cork city and Kinsale,' says Paddy.

Paddy can be justifiably proud of his status in Cork – his name was chosen, above that of his idol Louis Armstrong, when a Cork hotel wanted to name its bar after a jazz icon. Paddy laughs out loud, however, at any suggestion that he would ever upstage his hero. 'The general manager of the Blarney Park hotel, Gerry O'Connor, rang me, saying they were working on having a jazz theme for their new bar. They were going to call it The Louis Armstrong Bar, which I thought was great. But then he said they had changed their minds, and were wondering if it would be okay to call it The Paddy Cole Bar instead. I was flabbergasted, and replied, "Louis would be turning in his grave if he heard that." But I said I was honoured that they would even think of doing so.

'Anyway, they gathered a lot of photographs and memorabilia from my career and displayed them around the walls of the bar. We went down for the official opening, and there was lots of music. It was a great night. Joe Mac, my old buddy from The Dixies Showband, came along and played with us. He also played with Billy Crosbie's band from time to time. The Cork people just love Joe Mac – apart from being such a fun character, he is also a great drummer. Because Joe is such a funny person, many people don't realise what a great musician, singer and entertainer he also is.

'I met Louis Armstrong once in Dublin, when he played at the Adelphi. It was great to have a photo taken with a real star! Sean "the spoofer" Jordan, our road manager with The Capitol, was involved with the gig that Louis was playing in Dublin. He brought me backstage to meet him, and I was so thrilled about that. To this day I'm convinced that Louis Armstrong is the best trumpet player I ever heard. For ideas and technique and everything else, including hitting high notes, he was just unreal. To meet him and have a photo taken with him was wonderful.'

After the move back to Dublin, Paddy started doing a lot of corporate work for major companies, as well as playing 'High Society' at many high society weddings. But in parallel to those lucrative gigs, Paddy has helped raise hundreds of thousands of euro for charities over the years. Being able to help the most vulnerable in society, and those who are seriously ill, has given him the greatest buzz of all.

'One morning recently, while having a cup of coffee with Helen in the Sandymount hotel, a man from Kilkenny who I didn't know came up to me to say thanks. The man said that he would never forget the money we helped raised for the AWARE organisation at a function in Kilkenny, and that the reason they raised nearly €100,000 was because we played at the concert. But it wasn't just us – they also had an amazing auction at the gig, with companies donating stuff to sell. All of that money was also included in the proceeds that went to AWARE. It is nice when people walk up to you and say thanks for being part of something like that.

Above: Paddy, Humphrey Lyttelton and Jack Bayle, recording for
Pat Kenny's RTÉ radio show, 1990s.
Below: Willie Hickey, Paddy, Paul Sweeney and Tom Breslin, at
Narin and Portnoo Golf Club, August 2009.

Above: Paddy presents Deirdre Hughes, appeals director of The Friends of St Luke's, with the proceeds of ten years of Paddy's fundraising concerts at the National Concert Hall. Below: With Pat Boone, Donie Cassidy and Maxi, at the National Concert Hall, Dublin, mid-1990s.

'Also, every year for many years, we did a concert in the National Concert Hall for St Luke's cancer hospital. Over the course of the years, we raised a quarter of a million euro. They took me around the hospital campus on one occasion to show me the accommodation they had built with the funds that we raised. The accommodation is for people, especially from the country, who have a loved one in the Dublin hospital and need to stay overnight while visiting ill relatives. It was lovely to see that in some small way we had helped. To this day, I still help them out with certain events, including their annual "Bluebell Day". It is a fundraising day, and sometimes I give them a helping hand or mention it on the radio.

'For many years, we also did shows in the National Concert Hall for St Mary's hospital in Castleblayney. My late sister Sadie was a day patient there for a while. We opened an herb garden for them, with nice walks and all around it. Our fundraising also helped build a bit of an extension, where people could have some privacy with somebody who was terminally ill or nearing the end of their life.

'My sister Sadie was a deeply religious girl, who had polio when she was young. But at that time, nobody realised that she also had celiac disease, and was eating all the wrong foods for a long time. She lived with my mother and was so close to her that it would have broken my mother's heart if she knew Sadie had died before her. But God has strange ways of organising things, as my mam had Alzheimer's then and she never knew that her eldest child had passed away before her.'

Virtually all of Paddy's memories of going back to Castleblayney over the years are happy ones. But there are three exceptions: when his father passed away; and then his sister; and later his mother. Paddy has some sound advice for people regarding telling loved ones how much they mean to you: 'It was sad when my dad passed away first. It's only when I was listening to a song by Mike and the Mechanics that goes "say it now and tell it now" that those words seemed so relevant. If there is somebody you love, tell them now.

'In my era we never hugged our fathers or told them we loved them, because they would have thought we were head cases! It's only when people are gone that you think, why didn't I do or say such-and-such a thing? Nowadays, our grandchildren – before the Covid-19 pandemic – would be over hugging us when we meet. My sons and daughter do likewise, and do so unashamedly. It's wonderful that the young people are like that now – it's so different to our time growing up.'

Paddy believes in doing good deeds, and in kind words and actions from the heart. A certain heart charity is also close to his heart – he has done sponsored walks abroad for the Irish Heart Foundation in America, South Africa and Argentina. 'It was all fundraising for them, and those of us involved paid our fares to go on those walks. Apart from doing all the walks, I would always bring a clarinet with me for a singsong and a session each night wherever we stayed. It is nice to have been able to help such worthy causes. I am also an ambassador now for the Make A Wish Foundation, which is for terminally ill children. It would just break your heart to see how ill some of those little children are. We had a Paddy Cole Golf Day last year and raised a lot of money for them also.

Chapter 11

A Very Sobering Cancer Scare

Paddy always adhered to his father's advice never to drink before going on stage, but having a few pints afterwards was a different matter. However, he never drank spirits, and claims to have been 'cured' of that notion early in his career by a former Taoiseach.

'The late Albert Reynolds didn't help me give up drinking completely, but he certainly cured me from drinking shorts. We were going to a gig in Muff during my Capitol career, but due to the deaths of members of a Derry musical family in a crash, the dance was cancelled. Many Derry fans went to the Donegal ballroom, but we decided it would be inappropriate to go there after such a tragedy. The promoter, Jim McIvor, was in complete agreement.

'So, we turned back towards Dublin, and stopped off in Longford. It was early in the afternoon and some of the other boys were having drinks. I had a few bottles of stout, which was what I was drinking at that time. Some of the lads were drinking brandy, and I decided to try it, as I never drank brandy before.

'Albert Reynolds, who later became Taoiseach and was a dance promoter at that time and a non-drinker, bought us some drinks. He looked at me in a quizzical manner and said something like, "So you like brandy," and he just poured brandy into me that day. I was never as sick in my life as I was after that. In fact, I think I was sick for days after it. It was afterwards that he said to me he knew I wasn't a drinker of shorts. "I saw you were not a drinker of spirits, and I wanted to show you the after-effects," said Albert. It was a lesson that lasted for life. Even in Vegas, it was pints of beer that I would drink mostly, while others were knocking back shorts.'

Paddy says that he was a 'bad drinker', and he explains what he means by that. 'I would sit and drink after a gig, sometimes with people that I didn't even know. The next day I would be asking myself, who were those people I was drinking with last night?'

In later years, when playing the regular gigs in the Harcourt hotel, he really became aware of the serious health dangers of drink. 'I got this bad throat infection and during some tests at the Ear, Nose and Throat Hospital, some nodules were discovered on my vocal cords. During the examination, and unknown to me, they took away some tissue from my throat for analysis. That resulted in me being unable to talk properly for weeks, and also meant that I couldn't do the gigs.

'The specialist said that he didn't think it was cancer, but if it was, they had probably got it at an early stage. That frightened the life out of me as I was lying in a bed in a recovery room. Every time now when I drive down

Adelaide Road in Dublin, I look at a tree that was outside the window of that recovery room. I was looking at that tree from inside the window, and thinking of the things I needed to do if I got bad news. It would be a week before I would hear the results of the analysis of the tissue, and I was saying to myself that this would be an awfully long week.

'Luckily for me, there was a lady named Chrissie Murphy, who was a matron in the hospital and was originally from Castleblayney. She was delighted to see me and recognised how worried I was about the tests. A few days afterwards, Chrissie phoned me. Warning me not to say anything when going in for the results, she said I had got the all-clear.

'I thanked God, and I thanked Chrissie. And when I went in to meet the specialist, I pretended I knew nothing, to save any problems or embarrassment for Chrissie. The consultant said to me at that stage not to take any alcoholic drink for four or five weeks, because it would impair the healing process. I followed that instruction, and I am off the drink since, and that's twenty-eight or twenty-nine years ago.

'That was no big deal, and I never went to any Alcoholics Anonymous meetings or anything like that. But to be honest, it was then I realised that people attending my gigs were buying me so many pints! One night after going back playing at the Harcourt hotel, I looked around and there was a row of pints sitting on the stage behind me. While it was my policy never to drink before going on stage, I felt at the jazz gigs that I had to have a pint from time to time. But I never drank after that cancer scare, and it changed my life. I am in no doubt whatsoever, that if I had not done so, I wouldn't still be here today.

'After the health scare, I would walk away from playing at many venues, leaving a row of pints on the stage with brown, flat heads, still standing untouched.

I saw a lot of my friends in show business, and others who were not in the business, die young from alcohol-related issues, and that was so sad to see.'

It is worth noting that another star who echoed the actions of Paddy Cole was his former colleague, the late Brendan Bowyer. In an interview with Barry Egan in the *Sunday Independent* in 2010, Brendan says being warned by his doctor that drink was killing him fast was the shock he needed. Even an earlier multi-vehicle car crash in Las Vegas, resulting in Brendan being arrested and put in a jail cell for drunk driving, had failed to stop his drinking. 'When I was behind bars for a while, I thought I could have killed any of those four people. I tried to quit. It wasn't happening. I was getting the shakes, so I gradually came back into it again.'

Brendan also states in the interview that his wife Stella insisted on that vital check-up by the family doctor, and insisted on getting him into a rehabilitation centre. 'She arranged with the doctor for that intervention. I think she felt that I was killing myself.' Brendan, who passed away at eighty-one in June 2020, continued entertaining, but never touched alcohol again for the last thirty-seven years of his life.

Paddy, who worked with his former colleague again during some of the showband reunion tours in recent decades, admired Brendan's determination to stay off alcohol. 'No matter where we were touring, Brendan made sure never to miss attending weekly meetings of Alcoholics Anonymous.'

Like many singers, musicians and movie stars, people such as Paddy, or the late Brendan Bowyer, were in a business where excessive drinking was a real hazard. But there was no time for drinking when making a movie, as Paddy was to find out. He had a taste of movie work, albeit briefly, during the 1990s. He laughs loudly about his fleeting foray into film.

'It was enjoyable, but it was tough work, as I was also doing gigs at the time and might have to be on the film set at five in the morning.

'The movie was "Hear My Song", the life story of singer Josef Locke. Amazingly, Peter Chelsom, who directed it, now listens to my radio programme every Sunday in Los Angeles. He said that when he was flicking through radio channels, he heard this voice and said, "Oh no! It couldn't be Paddy Cole." He thought I was back to haunt him! He is a great guy, and keeps in touch with me all the time, but I had only three words to say in that movie. I played the clarinet, and my acting role was as a friend of Josef Locke.

'The only words I had to say were, "She never left." That was my line, after another actor had said, "Is the boat still at such-and-such a harbour?" I had to say, "She never left." I used to drive all the boys in the band crazy by saying, "Think of all the different ways you can say, 'She never left.'" It can be fast or with a slow drawl, or a dozen other ways to say it with feeling. My band colleagues would be muttering among themselves that I had lost the plot or that I thought I was John Wayne. I got some slagging about that,' laughs Paddy.

Paddy's singing colleague Joe Cuddy and Reggie Lloyd from his band also had parts in the film. Ned Beatty played the part of Josef Locke, and Adrian Dunbar from Enniskillen, who played in showbands, was one of the actors. John Altman, a great saxophone player, was the musical director.

'I was at a charity golf event in the K-Club some years ago,' recalls Paddy, 'when to everyone's astonishment, a Hollywood actor ran across the floor and lifted me up in the air. He shouted, "She never left!" He had remembered me from the filming of the Josef Locke movie. It was a bit of fun playing that tiny part in the movie, but it was a short-lived film career,' he laughs. Following a week's filming, many of the stars and crew would join him in the Harcourt hotel 'for a singing session' on Sunday nights.

Paddy has great memories of another great music session with one of America's most famous singers and pianists, Harry Connick Jnr, after he played for his father Harry Connick Snr's wedding. Harry Snr's first wife died in 1981, and he married Londa Jean Matherne in Ireland on 25 March 1995. 'Harry Connick Snr was a musician as well as being the State Attorney in New Orleans, where he heard me playing in one of the clubs. He and his new bride were coming to Ireland to Adare Manor, and he asked myself and the band to play at their wedding reception.

'Several planes with guests flew in from America for the event, including Harry Jnr and his band plus many Hollywood celebrities. There were also people there that I knew from playing in the clubs of New Orleans. We had a great day and night in Adare Manor. I was honoured to be asked to play at it, and Harry Snr and Jnr came up and played with us for a few numbers.'

As Harry Connick Jnr is a renowned pianist, with more number 1 albums than any other artist in American jazz chart history, everybody expected him to play the piano at Adare Manor. Not so, says Paddy. 'He just wanted to play the drums with us, which seemed strange at the time. Subsequently, I saw him at a concert in the 3Arena, and he also insisted on playing the drums during part of that gig. I thought it was weird, because he had a brilliant drummer. With all due respect to Harry Connick Jnr, who is a brilliant pianist, composer and actor, he wasn't a brilliant drummer. While the drumming seemed to be all part of a gimmick, I couldn't understand it.

'Also, he may have missed the boat here in Ireland with that live show, as he had only a four- or five-piece group, if memory serves me correctly. But Michael Bublé came in shortly afterwards with a big band and orchestra and became a megastar here. The night we saw Harry Jnr in the 3Arena, his smaller group played a lot of self-indulgent stuff. We were expecting him with a good-size big band and brass section, and singing all the swing stuff, but he wasn't. He seemed to be trying to reinvent himself and, to me anyway, it didn't work . But both Harry Snr and Jnr were nice people, and we got on great with them on our trips to New Orleans.'

That was all in 1995. Over a dozen years later, in 2008, Paddy made it back into the pop charts with his *King of the Swingers* album. That album might never have happened if not for the persistence of his manager at the time, Noel Carty. 'He is one of the true blues, and still a great buddy of mine.

'None of the record labels were interested in the album when we had it recorded. We went to a fellow named Willie Kavanagh, who was the chief at one of the major record labels and he said, "No, it wouldn't sell a dozen copies." But Noel Carty didn't give up, and he went to RTÉ, suggesting that they should consider it for their label. They agreed, as it was a new genre of music for them to be involved with on record. Shortly after its release, *King of the Swingers* was in the pop charts alongside many international names. Only for the persistence of Noel Carty, that album would probably never even have been released, let alone become a chart hit,' says Paddy.

An earlier album, titled *Celtic Rendezvous*, was also successful, but Paddy says that some of the tunes were 'counter-productive' when played at dances. 'I did it in Frank McNamara's studio in Meath. I recorded that before Phil Coulter started recording his albums of Celtic tunes. But when playing at dances and someone asked me to play "My Lagan Love" – if ever you wanted to kill a gig, that was the way to do it,' laughs Paddy. However, while not great for dances, the album still opened a new market for him among buyers of Irish music.

A lifetime ambition was fulfilled for Paddy as he brought his own band
to New Orleans, the great melting pot of jazz, in the mid-1990s.

The Paddy Cole Band in action in New Orleans, mid-1990s, with Jimmy LaRocca on trumpet.

Above: Final night of the 2015 Showband Reunion Tour,
Waterfront Theatre, Belfast.
Below: A tribute to Connie Lynch, at the Roselawn Lounge, Dublin:
Jimmy Magee, Paddy, Anne Lynch, Connie Lynch, Carol Hanna, Noel Carty.

Receiving a Hall of Fame award, along with Michael Flatley.

Another venture that opened new doors for Paddy's music was his *Craic'n'Cole* TV series on RTÉ 1 in 1995. 'John McColgan contacted me, saying that Tyrone Productions had been in touch with RTÉ about this type of TV show. We did it from different places around Ireland, using the outside broadcast unit. Shows were filmed in Monaghan, Cork, Athlone and Galway, and we had special guests each night. I hadn't much of a say regarding the guests, as that was done by a production team. If I had, I might have put some others on as well. But John was brilliant to work with, and he did everything possible to ensure that I was happy with the show.

'At the end of the series, he got in touch with me and said that we would be doing a follow-up series the next year. But the following year was a wonderful one for John McColgan and Tyrone Productions, because *Riverdance* came down on the world like a sheet of lightning. He told me afterwards that amid the euphoria of it all, he forgot to put the application in to RTÉ for our follow-up TV series. It was even on the provisional schedule for RTÉ the next year, but when they got no application, the RTÉ people thought we weren't interested.

'John phoned me and apologised profusely. He said there was another studio-based show that RTÉ would offer me, with a three-piece group and guest. But after the first series being so good with a twelve-piece big band, I declined. John and I are still great friends to this day.'

Paddy also became great friends with Michael Flatley of *Riverdance* and *Lord of the Dance* fame. 'We got music awards on the same night, at a televised show from the National Concert Hall. Michael got his award for *Riverdance*, and I got the Hall of Fame award, presented by Ronan Keating of Boyzone. We had a wonderful night, and I was there again with him after he left *Riverdance* and went on to create *Lord of the Dance*. I was in his company with a few other guys in a bar in Dublin, and we were advising him to stay with *Riverdance*. But he left anyway and made a huge success of *Lord of the Dance*. Both shows are still going stronger than ever.'

Since his *Craic'n'Cole* series, Paddy has become a regular on countless other TV shows, including the *Late Late Show*, the show *Twink* and many more. One of the more recent ones was *Opry le Daniel*, the bilingual show presented by Daniel O'Donnell from Derry on TG4. 'We used a little bit of *Gaeilge*, but it was mostly in English. Daniel was one of the most professional people I have ever worked with. Nothing is left to chance; everything is thought out and done properly. He had a great band also on that show, including two brilliant brass players – Ronan Dooney was on trumpet, and he played on the soundtrack of *The Commitments* film, while Carl Geraghty on sax has played with everyone from Kenny Rogers to Michael Jackson.

'Daniel is a very honest and unassuming guy for a man who has conquered the world with his own genre of music. The crowds that he does in America, Australia and elsewhere are unbelievable. He is a lovely person, and sometimes Helen and I meet him and Majella in Tenerife. They always

Daniel O'Donnell, Brian McGill and Paddy in Tenerife.

Sean Ashmore, CEO of Sunshine Radio, holds the Radio Station of the Year Award, 2019.

....

invite Helen and me out for a meal or we might meet them in the Hole in the Wall bar, where singer Fergal Flaherty plays,' says Paddy.

Just as Daniel has slipped with ease into presenting TV shows, Paddy moved with equal aplomb into radio presenting. He is on Dublin's Sunshine Radio (106.8FM) every Sunday morning from 9 to 11. 'Seán Ashmore, CEO of the radio station, asked me would I do the show almost fifteen years ago. I wasn't that keen at first, and said that I didn't want to be putting on a pseudo-American accent. I also asked him if I would have the freedom to pick the music. He agreed, and it was an hour-long show at first.

'He said to try it for three months and see how it works out. That reminded me of when I was asked to try out the gig in the Harcourt hotel for three months, and so I said I would give it a go. It was extended to two hours, and I still enjoy doing it, almost fifteen years later.

'I'm enjoying it even more now, because Joe Harrington produces the programme and he is excellent. He has been in radio all his life, and we have a great bit of banter and craic – so much so that when a little old lady saw me in Ranelagh recently, she first said, "Ah! Paddy, how are ya?" but then her expression changed. "I used to think you were a nice fella, until I heard the hard time you gave to Joe last week." It seems I said something to Joe on the show the week before that didn't go down very well with her.

'There is a bit of controversy now and again, and people write in to complain about one of us being too hard on the other. They might write in to say that Joe was too hard on me and he should stay quiet. Others write in and say that I was rude to Joe, but of course it's all a bit of fun and Joe and I get on very well. We have a bit of banter going on and it has reached the stage now where people expect that from us. Also, I had been trying out a comedy slot in the past, and now Noel V Ginnity is the most popular comedian on the show.'

Paddy tried to be a comedian, but it didn't work, and some of his most avid listeners among the Dublin taxi driver community were quick to tell him so. In your mind's eye, perhaps you can picture the scene: It's a lazy, sunny Sunday afternoon on Baggot Street, Dublin. Paddy is walking along after doing his show. He may be feeling a bit smug that his attempts at telling jokes are adding to the mix of his programmes. Suddenly the relative stillness of the sidewalk is shattered by a shout from a nearby taxi rank. It quickly removes any of Paddy's smugness. 'One of the taxi drivers said, loud enough for all his colleagues and all the street to hear, "Paddy, you play great music on that show, but your jokes are brutal. That's even to the comedians among us," added the unofficial taxi spokesperson. It wasn't a busy morning for them, and so most of the others shouted, "He's right, Paddy, ya know." That instantly put an end to any aspirations I had to being a comedian! So, any time I tell a joke or relay a joke now on the show, I preface it by saying it is with apologies to the taxi drivers,' laughs Paddy.

With Joe Harrington, producer of 'The Paddy Cole Show'.

Paddy, Noel V Ginnity and George Hunter.

Paddy has a huge following on Facebook for his radio programme. He wasn't on Facebook himself at the start, but the numbers were so big that he had to sign up to it. 'I was reluctant, as I am not on Twitter or any of those sites. But now I have a few thousand people who say they are my friends on Facebook – but sure I hardly know any of them,' he laughs. He always puts up posts on Facebook on Saturdays previewing what he will have on the show the following day.

On the radio show, Paddy has a big band slot, the songs from the shows slot and the comedy slot. He says the discs he plays are a very mixed musical bag. He laughs out loud when asked if he plays much modern pop stuff, or if he would ever consider recording an instrumental album of current chart hits. 'I don't think that people would expect to hear me playing something by Madonna! The enthusiasm wouldn't be there now for something like that at this stage in the game.'

Paddy is not enthusiastic about recording another album either. 'I don't think I will, even though George Hunter, who manages Dickie Rock and does the dates for me, has suggested an album. When John Prine died, I recorded "Stay A Little Longer", which was a type of country number, but I did a more up-tempo, rocky version. I put a sax solo into it, and George thought it was great. Others have said I could do some Doug Kershaw Cajun numbers, and put in a few sax solos in them. But, while I don't want to sound as if I'm throwing in the towel regarding recordings, you still need to be very enthusiastic about any project. That enthusiasm needs to be there.

'When I played "Ag Críost an Síol" at Brendan Grace's funeral, Marty Whelan said to me afterwards it was beautiful, and that I should record it. Subsequently others said the same after I played the same piece on the clarinet at funerals of a few other friends. If it was years ago, I might be rushing into a studio. But nowadays I say that Seán Ó Riada, the RTÉ Orchestra and others have done it all, and done it better than I would.

'Also, after the Covid-19 pandemic, and while I hope that I am wrong, I can't see many people of my agegroup ever doing live gigs again. George Hunter had a concert tour lined up for me at the end of 2020, but all that is on hold now. I'm still enthusiastic about playing, but recording? Well, I don't think so. Everybody has a different idea about what I should record.

'I was asked to send a congratulations message recently to a couple that we know on their fiftieth wedding anniversary. Just to spice it up a bit, I also played a tune on it, without any backing. They messaged me back to say it was brilliant, and that I should record that tune, exactly as it was. But it's different going into a studio and doing it with backing and arrangements and other musicians, compared to playing it in your sitting room and recording it on an iPhone,' he laughs.

One of Paddy's proudest moments was in 2019, when a massive mural of him playing the saxophone was unveiled on a two-storey gable beside his old home. The mural looks down upon the street opposite where Paddy was raised. 'It was a fantastic event, and an emotional one too, as I remembered my parents and my older sister who were no longer there to see it. The Castleblayney Regeneration Group contacted me with the idea. They already have a Wall of Fame in the town that all of us local musicians are on. It also has pictures of other musicians who have made Castleblayney their home.

'When Annmarie McHugh from the group asked me to attend a meeting about it, I thought they might be putting a different small picture on the Wall of Fame. She took me to the site of a relatively new building where the old customs post used to be. I said, what part of that gable wall is the picture going on? She shocked me when she replied that it would cover the entire two-storey gable of the building.

'They put it out to tender for different artists to come up with a design, and one who applied was a Japanese artist. I was delighted that his interpretation didn't get it – not for any bad reason, but because he had all sorts of spaceships flying across the skies, and I was the pilot in them with stars and moons all around me. He really was putting me up there among the stars,' laughs Paddy. 'Anyway, the artist Jonathan Lynn did an excellent job, and he kept in touch with me at all stages. He wanted to know about the notes on the sax, and what way I would hold it. He was intent on making sure that every aspect of it was right. Jonathan has painted murals in Paris, London, Madrid and now Castleblayney!

'On the day of the unveiling, Helen and I, as well as our son Pat and our grandchildren, travelled down from Dublin for the event. Others who did so included my great friends Noel V Ginnity, Paul Sweeney, Mick Sherry and Tom Breslin. When we arrived in 'Blayney, the place was packed. My sisters were all there as well, and there was a band playing as the people were arriving.

'Then they pulled back this tarpaulin-type covering that had been hiding the mural and a cheer went up. Robert Irwin, who managed Big Tom and The Travellers at one time, did the introduction, and he did it so well. Then I said a few words of thanks to Annmarie McHugh and the whole committee and all of the others involved. It was a great honour, because the old saying is that a prophet is never accepted in his own land, but it was so nice to be accepted and shown to be accepted in my own hometown.

'I had some regrets that my father and mother and sister Sadie were not there to see it. They would have been thrilled to bits. But, on the way into Castleblayney that day, I went to the cemetery and spoke to them for about fifteen minutes. In my mind, I told them that this was happening, and I told my dad how much I appreciated him teaching me to play. I thanked my mother for all the sacrifices they made for me over the years, and my sister Sadie for being so supportive of my music career. I had my own chat with them. Then I put all that out of my head and moved off down the town to the celebration. Otherwise I might have been too overcome with emotion at the unveiling.

'On a lighter note, somebody asked me why I thought they had put the mural up on that gable. I replied that perhaps it's a good thing to aim at for the kids when they are lifting sods and throwing them at the wall – they can throw them at me instead.'

Chapter 12

'Do You Feel Like an Orange?' 'No. Do I Look Like One?'

To put it crudely, it was a bit like a group of farmers rushing across a field to catch their favourite sheep flocked against a wall on the other side. The men were waiting and eying up the fairest in the flock. When Paddy and the band started playing, there was a shemozzle across the dance floor to grab the female most likely. To quote Paddy's friend, the singing star Big Tom, 'If you didn't get the one you wanted then you wanted the one you got!'

The first words were, 'Will ya dance?' If she even nodded, before some-body else in the swirling, sweating, heaving crowd swept her off her feet, the courting had begun. Or maybe it hadn't! In the drink-free, dusty dance-halls and marquees of post-Second World War Ireland, and in Irish dance halls abroad, this was a typical scene, even up to the 1980s.

Usually showbands such as those Paddy Cole was in played a set of fast dances first, so that the dash across the dancefloor could start. Then, three tunes in, the crunch came, when a slow set of dances was announced. If the potential suitor seemed suitable to the fair maiden, she might agree to get up closer and more personal for the slow set. But if not, the amorous advances of the lovelorn lad were dismissed instantly. He went back to his corner with his tail between his legs!

However, if he thought he was getting lucky in love, and she stayed on for the slow set, then the real killer chat-up line was uttered. 'Do you feel like an orange?' But alas! The lass might swiftly reply, 'No! Do I look like one?' and scurry across the floor back to her female friends. The 'orange' in question would be a non-alcoholic fizzy drink sold at the mineral bar. If the girl agreed, but afterwards wanted to go back dancing, or watching musicians such as Paddy play, even for the following two hours, the fellow had to oblige.

On the way home, especially if they were travelling by bicycle, he might be lucky enough to have a roll in some hayshed, or hayfield if it was summer, with the lady of his dreams! This scenario is powerfully described in Vin-cent Power's brilliant 1990 book about the ballrooms and the showbands *Send 'em Home Sweatin'*.

Those days of showbands and dancehalls reflect a very different Ireland, an Ireland of a bygone age. But they were the reality for many, and were a part of the social history of Ireland, especially rural Ireland. The dances were often operated by parish priests, who would sometimes use an umbrella to prise people apart on the dancefloor – social distancing, decades before Covid-19!

Paddy Cole's music has been a part of the soundtrack over decades of change in a chameleon country. He could have become a Garda or a butcher or an electrician. Having wondered at times, when playing in cold, half-empty dancehalls, why he hadn't chosen another career path, octogenarian Paddy says he is glad he didn't.

'My singing colleague, the late Sonny Knowles, used to say sometimes, "Two more years and I could have been a plumber." Everybody who has paid their dues in show business has had thoughts about why they didn't follow another career path. I often feel sorry for young people who are whisked from obscurity to stardom overnight. Then, when they fade off the scene and are gone for good, they must become very disillusioned. But for somebody who has paid their dues over the years, they know how to hop right back up again after a fall.

'There is nobody in show business who hasn't had bad nights, with bad crowds. All you can do is go on stage, do the gig, do your best, and irrespective of there being twenty or 2,000 there, the show must go on,' says Paddy.

Highlights for him included playing at The London Palladium and being invited to play, with his own Dixieland band, in New Orleans. 'It's the home of Dixieland, and to be subsequently invited back six times to play there was a great honour. Being presented by Ronan Keating with the Hall of Fame Award in Ireland's National Concert Hall was another great honour. On a personal side, I must thank my wife Helen and my children and grandchildren, as well as all my sisters, for being so supportive of my career.'

Paddy has travelled a long way, from the drudgery of playing small, dimly lit rural halls to the bright lights of Vegas and beyond. Even being booed at one highlight event in Vegas was enjoyable for Paddy, as he explains: 'We were taken to meet Cassius Clay – later Muhammad Ali – before his fight with Joe Bugner. But when we were announced as the Irish showband, there to support Cassius, we were booed by the British fans of his opponent Joe Bugner. We got to meet Cassius through the good offices of Gene Kilroy, who was of Irish descent and was one of his right-hand men.

'He wanted us there to meet Cassius at an afternoon session in Vegas while he was training for the fight. There were about 5,000 paid-in boxing enthusiasts there, just to watch him training. He never took a break. As one sparring partner after another came in, he just kept boxing, for well over an hour. Then the MC said they wanted to welcome some of Cassius Clay's biggest fans, the Irish showband. A big "Boo!" went up, as it was mostly British fans of Joe Bugner in that crowd. When Gene Kilroy heard this, he invited us up into the ring to meet Cassius Clay, and that really killed them completely,' he laughs.

Paddy and the band also met the boxer Joe Louis, but he said that wasn't as euphoric. 'He ended up as a host at Caesar's Palace, and that was sad to see, as all he was doing there was being available to be photographed with fans. We were brought up to have our photo taken with him and to have a chat with him by our bosses from the Stardust club. He was probably getting paid well by Caesar's Palace to do this, but I thought he was dejected-looking. While chatting with him, I also felt that it was degrading for a man who had been such a star to be doing this sort of hotel work.'

Playing in Dubai was another highlight of Paddy's professional life, almost on a par with Vegas. 'We were brought out at first by the Irish living

Tom Dunphy, TJ Byrne, Muhammad Ali, Brendan Bowyer and Paddy,
before the Joe Bugner fight.

in Dubai, to play at a St Patrick's Day show there. Then the following year, we were booked for two weeks out there. We played in Doha, Dubai, Abu Dhabi and other places across the Middle East. They were mostly outside gigs at the sides of swimming pools in the big hotels, and the audiences were also mostly Irish and British plus a few Arabic people.'

The Arabic attendance may have been influenced to come and see Paddy because they watched his young sister Lucia present a popular show on TV there at that time. 'It was great to go there at a time when my sister Lucia was in Doha, where she had her own TV and radio shows. She was hugely popular, like Qatar's answer to Gay Byrne or Ryan Tubridy. When I was with her in some of the big department stores, the bosses and customers would come up to her and address her as "Miss Lucia". She was a great help to us when we were touring out there.'

Paddy has experienced disappointments in life too. But he is philosophical about this, saying that you realise, as you get older, that not everything works out the way you want it to. 'I don't mind admitting that I worked hard for anything that I've got in life. At one stage, I was running the bar and working there, while also driving six nights a week between Castleblayney and Dublin, three weeks at a time.

Of course, there were also some small disappointments during my show business career. I might say, "Why did this guy drop me off that show?" and niggly little things like that. But the most disappointing things of all in life were discovering that people I thought were true friends, and who I trusted, weren't friends at all. That is more sad than disappointing, but it happens to everybody, unfortunately. You will have lots of acquaintances, and others who seem closer until you have a problem, and then you know your true friends.

'There is one man living here in Dublin who has been one of my truest friends to this day, and that is Mick Sherry. We meet regularly for coffee and a chat. One of the saddest moments of my life happened when we were away in Vegas and his son, Simon, was killed in a freak accident at the age of fifteen. We were at Barry McGuigan's World Championship boxing match in Las Vegas, which Barry lost, but that loss was dwarfed into insignificance when we heard of young Simon's death. We had to make a mad rush to get charter flights home, and after reaching New York, I managed to get to Dublin. Helen met me at the airport, having driven from Castleblayney, with the clarinet. There was another mad rush to reach the church to play a piece at the Mass. Events such as that bring you down to earth very quickly.'

Sport remains a big hobby for Paddy, especially golf, which he plays in Dublin and Lahinch, where he has a holiday home. He is also a big Gaelic football fan. However, there seems to be divided loyalty regarding which football team he supports – his native Monaghan or Dublin where he is domiciled. He laughs as he explains: 'Well, I support both at times. Away back in my early days, Dublin star Paddy Cullen became a great fan of The Capitol Showband. So also was Jimmy Keaveney and later Tony Hanahoe, Brian Mullins and all those Dublin footballers.

'When Dublin won the first All-Ireland that Paddy Cullen was involved in, he has referred to my support on the DVD filmed about that win. I was the first man over the small wall in Croke Park to lift him up in the air. I followed the Dubs non-stop, and we have a photo of our sons Pearse and Pat sitting in the Sam Maguire Cup at the school in Kilmacud where they were pupils. The players, Sean Doherty and Paddy Cullen brought the cup to the school. But when they asked if Pearse and Pat Cole were in the class-room, the boys thought they were being sought for doing something wrong!

Paddy Cullen (goalie) and Seán Doherty (captain) of Dublin's 1974 All-Ireland-winning football team, with Pearse and Pat Cole and the Sam Maguire cup.

When we had the pub in Castleblayney, Paddy Cullen brought the cup there also and we had a great night.

'A great friend of mine, John Pardy, who manages the Iveagh Gardens hotel for the McGill family, often has the Dublin footballers there. John is also one of my golfing buddies. I was in that hotel shortly before their star player, Anton O'Toole, passed away. It was sad to see him on crutches that day. He was so fast on the field that he became known as the Blue Panther, and he was also a lovely person. They were all there that day, and I noticed that they were all well-built men, but also very well-mannered fellows. John Pardy would often phone me and say that players such as Jimmy Keaveney or Tony Hanahoe were coming in for coffee, and could I join them?

'I always got on great with the Dublin players, but of course, I have always followed Monaghan. The year they won the Ulster title, we were playing in the Four Seasons hotel in Monaghan that night. The whole team came in with the cup, and I borrowed the jersey of star player Nudie Hughes. When I arrived on stage wearing it, the place erupted. Nudie worked for us in the bar and what a brilliant player he was. I still go to Croke Park to see Monaghan play. Regarding winning All-Ireland titles, we're still looking for one-in-a-row,' he says with a laugh.

But if Monaghan were to meet Dublin in an All-Ireland final, who would he be cheering for? Paddy's unequivocal answer is, 'Monaghan, of course!' Because of that, he says his producer on the Sunshine Radio show, Joe Harrington, castigates him as being 'only a fair-weather Dublin supporter'. Paddy says he is lucky to have befriended top footballers from most Irish counties during his years following the sport.

While he obviously loves his work on radio, Paddy always seems at ease on TV too. But has this always been the case? 'Well, when I was doing the *Craic'n'Cole* show, that was a mind-boggler for me. Jack Bayle was doing the arrangements for the twelve- or fourteen-piece band, and I was interviewing all the guests. I had a music stand beside me with the arrangements for all the pieces while I was also interviewing the guests. I had to switch over in my mind, while reading the piece of music, to thinking about what I would say immediately afterwards, and that was a mind-boggler.

'Generally though, I enjoy television work and I am relaxed when doing it. I just say to myself that at any one time there is only one household looking at me, and not hundreds of thousands. So, you just do it as if you are talking to that one household. I've done hundreds of TV shows. I didn't realise that I had appeared on the *Late Late Show* over twenty times until Ryan Tubridy told me so. We met one day in Dalkey in Dublin, where we were both attending the same dentist. Ryan said to me that they were going to have a fiftieth anniversary of the *Late Late Show*, and people that had made over twenty or twenty-five appearances would be automatically invited. I said that sounds great. But when Ryan said that I was in that group, I was pleasantly surprised. I went along that night and really enjoyed it. I was sitting with Twink, Red Hurley, Daniel O'Donnell and Dickie Rock, I think.

'I also had a lot of appearances on *Live at 3* on RTÉ when Noel Smith was a producer. He knew the business backways. He was the ultimate professional and knew what sort of acts suited the afternoon viewers. At one stage, we were the resident band on the show every Wednesday. Sadly, a lot of the other guys in the business that were so good to us – such as Larry Gogan and Gay Byrne, to name but two – are gone.'

Paddy Cole is known as the King of the Swingers by his fans and everybody in show business in Ireland, but how did he get that name? 'I think it was my former manager, Noel Carty, who came up with that name when we were releasing our album in 2008. That track was on the album and Noel suggested it as a good name for the CD. The name has stuck with me ever since. Even one of Brendan O'Carroll's TV shows, *Mrs Brown's Boys*, mentioned me as King of the Swingers. Mrs Brown [aka Brendan] was in a pub, talking about a party they were planning, and they were pretending not to know what a swingers' party was. Suddenly Mrs Brown said, "We should get Paddy Cole, because he is the King of the Swingers," and everybody laughed at the double meaning of that.'

Brendan has told him since that they were considering him for an appearance on the top-rated TV show at one stage. 'Brendan came over to me after Brendan Grace's funeral and said so. He said they had been considering having the band and myself play in the corner of a pub for the swingers' party. He took a fit of laughing when he was telling me. But due to some production changes to that show, it never happened.'

There is more than a double meaning to his stage name – there is also a third meaning, as Paddy explains: 'Dermot Gilleece, the golf correspondent, wrote a book about the game, and he signed my copy "to the King of the Swingers". He added, "Keep swinging outdoors and indoors," which was nice.'

Raising money for GOAL: Father D'Arcy, John O'Shea, Derek Dean, Brendan O'Brien, Paddy, Joe Dolan, Joe Mac, Sonny Knowles, Sean Dunphy, Earl Gill, Eileen Kelly, Frankie McBride and Eamon Monahan (on piano).

A lot of Paddy's golfing pals at Lahinch Golf Club are also musicians and they often have an 'unplugged session' after a game. 'We also did a session on the evening of the Irish Open, when the golfing was over. The clubhouse was packed, and we played for an hour or so there just for the craic and a bit of a party.'

Trout fishing was one of Paddy's hobbies since childhood. He doesn't get to do it anymore, but hopes to take it up again. 'I still have all the rods, reels, flies and lines, everything. Every year, I say that I must get back to doing some trout fishing, because I always enjoyed it.'

Paddy also likes to read a lot, on topics such as history and crime, as well as gangster stories. 'I am currently reading three books, and I am completely confusing myself at times. I have the wrong people from one book shooting people that are characters in the other book,' he laughs. One book that he is reading 'for the third time' is *A Confederacy of Dunces* by John Kennedy Toole. 'He was a young man who lived in New Orleans, and it was published posthumously, as he committed suicide and died in his twenties. It is one of the best books I have ever read.'

Paddy has been the voluntary Chairman of the Recorded Artists, Actors and Performers (RAAP) organisation for the past eighteen years. 'We collect royalties and distribute them on behalf of our members. The organisation was formed in 2002, to ensure that Irish performers get their fair share if their works are played on the air. We have reciprocal arrangements with similar societies in America, Germany and other countries. We also collect money for airplay given to Irish artists in other countries, and we pass this on to the acts here. Everybody on the Board is doing it on a voluntary basis, and we keep administrative costs as low as possible.'

Above: Paddy with Ronan Collins.
Below: With Taoiseach Bertie Ahern at the *Late Late Show*, around 2007.

Above: Paul McGinley with the Ryder Cup, 2002.
Below: Terry Wogan, Paddy and Paddy Reilly,
before the Terry Wogan Golf Classic.

RAAP have done a lot of lobbying of politicians for fair play for artists and actors. The organisation is currently at the centre of a court case to get monies paid in Ireland to Irish artists, as Éanna Casey, CEO of the organisation, explained: 'Paddy has worked tirelessly, specifically on this campaign, to ensure that performers are paid when their works are broadcast or publicly performed. He has an invaluable wealth of experience and knowledge. His personal management skills are amazing, and that's what made him an ideal chairman for the organisation. On a personal note, he has been an amazing mentor for me over the years.'

Paddy and Helen are regular churchgoers, and their local priest in Haddington Road is Father Pat Claffey, a brother of Paul Claffey of Mid-West Radio, also a friend of Paddy and a well-known music promoter. Father Brian D'Arcy is another great friend, who Paddy says 'has looked after everybody in show business' over the years. 'Brian is a great guy who did some of our family weddings, and he is a very open-minded priest. I know a couple who were living together with a family, but their parents, who were a bit old-world like myself, would have preferred if they were married. When they approached their local priest, he stupidly wouldn't do the wedding ceremony. I asked Father Brian, and he had no issue doing it, in Mount Argus in Dublin, where he was a priest at that time. My former manager, the late Tony Loughman, and Monaghan footballer Nudie Hughes were among many music and sports people who helped Father Brian raise funds for Mount Argus when it needed massive refurbishment.'

Among gigs that Paddy and the band have played in recent years have been ones at the American and British embassies in Ireland. He also has great memories of playing at weddings for family members of former Taoiseach Charlie Haughey and his wife Maureen. But the

With friends at the Paddy Cole Golf Classic, Castleblayney:
Evan Henry, Paddy, Martin McArdle, Ignatius Murray, Mick Sherry.
Below: The Board of RAAP:
Back: CEO Éanna Casey, Ronan Keating, Andrew Basquille, Paddy;
Front: Alan McEvoy, Ciaran Goss, Wendy Vard, Ciaran Tourish, Mary Black, Ritchie Buckley

aftermath of one such wedding wasn't great for Paddy and the band: 'It was in a beautiful marquee put up in the grounds of the Haughey home in Kinsealy by Frank Fahy's company Eventus Marquees. There was an amazing water fountain feature in front of the house, and they constructed the marquee around that.

'Eamon Monahan said that he would like to come out during the meal and play a few pieces on the piano. He knows so many classical pieces and is so good on the piano that he was ideal for that. He spoke to the manager of the famous Walton's music store, and convinced him to give us the lend of a snow-white grand piano. But this was on the understanding that it came back without a scratch or a mark on it. Walton's big truck delivered the piano to the marquee, and Eamon played it at the reception and everything went off great.

'But we didn't realise that the marquee company were taking down the tent overnight until we got a dramatic phone call from Walton's shop the next morning. When the truck driver and his assistant went back out to collect the white piano, it wasn't completely white anymore. It was sitting in the middle of the field, with two cattle scratching their backsides up against it! There was hell to pay, and I think the piano had to go back to be resprayed and re-lacquered. The Walton's manager warned us never to come near the shop again for anything.'

While Paddy had a good friendship with the late Charlie Haughey, his relationship with another Taoiseach, the late Albert Reynolds, went back much further, back to his early showband days in fact. As stated in another chapter, Paddy credits Albert with stopping him from drinking brandy. When Paddy was a young musician, Albert and his brother Jim were operating dancehalls across the country. The Cloudland ballroom in Albert's hometown of Rooskey in Roscommon was the first of fourteen ballrooms operated throughout the country by the Reynolds brothers.

According to his obituary in August 2014 in the *Irish Times*, the Reynolds chain of ballrooms was constructed in tandem with the rise of the showbands. 'The growth of the company coincided with the dawn of the showband era and the Reynolds brothers brought leading bands such as the Clipper Carlton, Royal, Miami, Capitol to rural Ireland. Dancers turned up in droves.'

The obituary also states that among the international acts Albert brought in were Johnny Cash, Roy Orbison and Jim Reeves. It also claimed that he built his home, Mount Carmel in Longford, with the profits of a ten-day tour by Kenny Ball and his Jazzmen.

With both Paddy Cole and Albert Reynolds sharing an interest in jazz, it is no wonder that their friendship flourished over the years. But Paddy says he never thought back then that Albert would one day be a chief architect of the Good Friday Agreement, bringing an end to armed hostilities in Northern Ireland.

Paddy says that when they met during Albert's term as Taoiseach, they often talked about the peace process and how the showband scene helped with it. 'I asked Albert on one occasion, how did he get in contact with Ian Paisley to start that dialogue on the peace process, and he gave me this answer: He asked me if I remembered Sammy Barr, who owned the ballroom in Ballymena. I replied yes, and Albert told me that he did his "networking" through Sammy, who was a close friend of Ian Paisley.

'I would never have thought of doing that, but Albert did. He told Sammy that he would like to have a chat with Ian Paisley, "I said to him that I thought it was nearly time we were sitting down and talking about peace," said Albert.

Albert Reynolds says hello, 1990s, at the opening of 'Elegant John' in Dublin.

Sammy Barr chatted with Paisley, and he sent word back to Albert to say that it didn't suit him to talk at that juncture. But he assured him that he would do so later, which he did,' says Paddy.

'Albert was a great guy behind the scenes, and he knew how to network. To phone Sammy Barr, who was of the same persuasion as Paisley, was a typical example of that. The Reynolds brothers also treated us very well in their ballrooms, back at a time when we never imagined one of them would become Taoiseach.'

Paddy was also friendly with former Presidents Mary Robinson and Mary McAleese and current President Michael D Higgins long before any of them achieved high office in the Áras. 'Mary McAleese's husband Martin was a dentist in Crossmaglen, and we knew them for years. When Mary came to the Cork Jazz Festival, she was at our gig in the Blarney Park hotel. We had her playing the sax, with me supposedly showing her how. She also had us at the Áras for meals, and one such reception was attended by an amazing cross-section of people. There were Sinn Féin councillors as well as out-and-out unionist councillors. It showed me, that night, how much she was doing to bring people of different persuasions together.

'We were asked to play at a victory function in the Burlington hotel when Mary Robinson was elected President. Michael D is great, and I remember playing at a wedding that he was attending after his election, but I didn't know he was there. I was about to start the music when one of the boys in the band said, "The President is waving up at you." So I went to the table where he was standing and waving at me. It was lovely to meet him again, and he put his arms around me and gave me a big hug. He loves music and the Arts, and Michael D has done so much for our business.'

A pair of Presidents.
Above: Paddy and Helen with Mary Robinson in the Burlington Hotel,
where Paddy played to celebrate her election as President, 1990.
Below: Mary McAleese, Paddy, Martin McAleese, at Áras an Úachtaráin
for a concert for members of the rural community.

Paddy Cole says that show business has been good to him, and he has no intention of retiring from it. 'I cringe when I hear that word, "retirement". I want to ease back a bit, and pick and choose where and when I will play. But there is an old saying, "You don't stop because you get old; but you get old because you stop," and that is why I won't be stopping.'

So concluded this sprightly octogenarian who, though approaching his eighty-first birthday, remains 'Forever Young', to quote a Bob Dylan song. This is no Old King Cole, but a young-at-heart, perhaps forever young King Paddy Cole, truly Ireland's King of the Swingers.

Strange Times

Strange times that we live in, not advised to go out,
Not for papers or coffee, or the black pint of stout.
So, we sit in the garden and think of what we miss –
A walk by the sea, our grandchildren's kiss,
We miss meeting old friends, talk of times gone by,
When we'd solve the world's problems and tell the odd lie.

To jump in the car, and head to the Banner,
Golf in Lahinch, and a swim in Liscannor,
To go to rehearsal, to learn a new tune,
But now I stay home, and learn to cocoon.

Soon this will be over, and for that we can't wait.
We'll be up, dressed and ready, and first out the gate.
In the meantime, be patient, be positive, be brave
And think of the rules, and the lives we can save.

Paddy Cole, 2020

Acknowledgements

Tom Gilmore thanks Paddy Cole, Helen and family for their unwavering support and co-operation, and good humour, during work on this project.

Thanks to John McColgan of *Riverdance* fame for his wonderful and insightful foreword on the amazing life and times of Paddy Cole.

Sincere thanks to Tim Ryan, author of *Tell Roy Rogers I'm Not In*, for allowing me to 'feel free to quote away' from his book – much appreciated, Tim.

I would also like to mention Ann, Raymond, Louise and Matthew Quirke and Kelly Carty for their friendship and support. To the extended Collins family in Chester, for their love and inspiration, and in particular Michael Collins and Joei Chung who tried their hardest to teach me how to use Zoom!

Thanks to my 'other family' in Perth, Australia, to Sean Burke, Milltown and Tuam, and John Giblin, Galway, for their indispensable audio research.

My gratitude to the extended Gilmore families in counties Galway, Cork and Sligo, and to all others who encouraged this project, especially David Burke, Editor, and my colleagues in *The Tuam Herald*. Also, my colleagues in Galway Bay FM.

To the publishers, O'Brien Press, in particular Michael O'Brien and editor Eoin O'Brien, as well as Ivan O'Brien, who also tried valiantly to teach me Zoom! Also, to Ruth Heneghan and all in marketing and promotion.

Thanks to RTÉ, TG4, Spotlight TV, BBC, Virgin TV and the many other media outlets, local radio, TV and of course the print media whose interviews, reports and photographic coverage of Paddy Cole's career are referred to in the pages of this book. Apologies if I have inadvertently omitted anyone.

Above all else thanks to Paddy Cole for sharing the amazing story of his amazing showbiz life with us all.

Other Books from the O'Brien Press

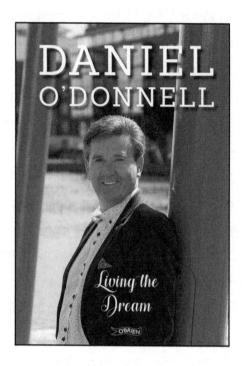

In Ireland, Daniel O'Donnell is more than just a singing star: he has reached the status of 'national treasure'. It has been a long journey for the boy from Kincasslagh, County Donegal, and in this updated autobiography, he tells his story with his customary sense of humour and down-to-earth charm.

Hardback ISBN: 978-1-84717-967-8
eBook ISBN: 978-1-84717-986-9

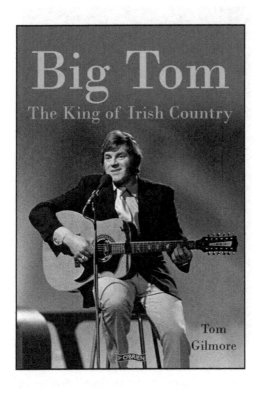

A tribute to Big Tom McBride, 'the Johnny Cash of Irish country music'. From labourer to music star, the journey of the singer who brought so much joy to fans at home and to emigrants abroad over five decades.

Tom Gilmore has interviewed family, friends and fans, as well as unearthing previously unpublished interviews with Big Tom himself.

Hardback ISBN: 978-1-78849-064-1
eBook ISBN: 978-1-78849-076-4

Philomena Begley takes us from her happy beginnings as a bread-man's daughter in Pomeroy through the devastating loss of her brother Patsy and the risks of touring Ireland at the height of the Troubles, right up to her fiftieth anniversary in show business in 2012 – her 'gold and silver days'.

Hardback ISBN: 978-1-84717-966-1
eBook ISBN: 978-1-84717-987-6

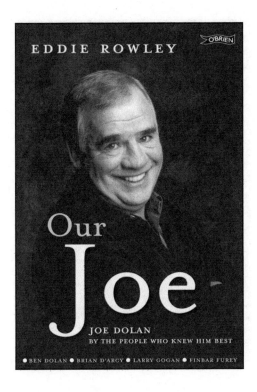

EDDIE ROWLEY

Our
Joe

JOE DOLAN
BY THE PEOPLE WHO KNEW HIM BEST

● BEN DOLAN ● BRIAN D'ARCY ● LARRY GOGAN ● FINBAR FUREY

Read the story of Joe Dolan through his own interviews and the memories and anecdotes of his family that vividly bring to life the essence of Joe. Jam-packed with a treasure trove of never-before-told stories that vividly bring to life the essence of Joe Dolan: the showbiz legend, the family man, the friend, the joker and the devil-may-care character who never forgot his roots or lost touch with his people despite enjoying fame and wealth beyond his dreams.

Paperback ISBN: 978-1-84717-275-4
eBook ISBN: 978-1-84717-460-4

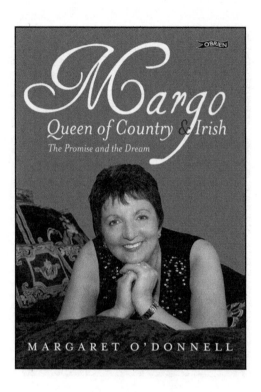

The official memoir of Margo O'Donnell, legendary Irish country music singer. For fifty years now the name 'Margo' has been synonymous with everything that is positive and enriching in Irish country music. This is the story of her life, the successes and difficult times, in her own words.

Hardback ISBN: 978-1-84717-674-5
eBook ISBN: 978-1-84717-702-5

The first book dedicated to the history of Horslips, the legendary pioneers of Celtic Rock. With a detailed timeline, exclusive interviews, previously unpublished photography and a wealth of memorabilia including handwritten lyrics and session notes.

Hardback ISBN: 978-1-84717-586-1

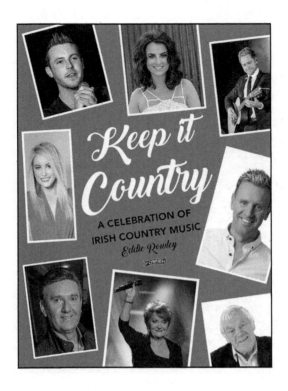

Immerse yourself in all that's great about the vibrant Irish country music scene. From Big Tom, Philomena and Daniel to Nathan, Lisa, Mike and many more, the leading lights of Irish country in their own words. This book is a must-have for Irish country music fans.

Hardback ISBN: 978-1-84717-968-5

As a performer and recording artist, Christy Moore has delighted Irish and international audiences alike. Now this unique collection presents the words and music of more than one hundred of the songs he has performed. From *Paddy on the Road* (1969) and *Prosperous* (1971), through the Planxty and Moving Hearts albums and back to his solo career with *The Time Has Come* (1983) and *Ride On* (1984), Christy Moore's music has always been innovative, influential and entertaining.

Paperback ISBN: 978-0-86322-063-0

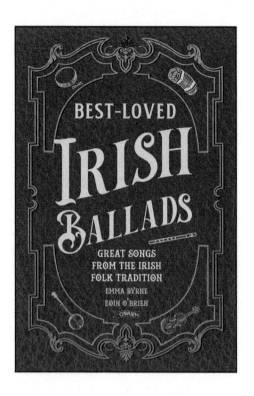

Songs to stir the soul and move the feet, raise a roar or bring a tear to the eye.

From 'Danny Boy' to 'Boulavogue' and more, this book celebrates the cream of Irish ballads, explaining the origins of each song, along with the words, melodies and chords. Illustrated with evocative photographs and woodcuts.

Hardback ISBN: 978-1-78849-220-1